HERBERT HOOVER
1874 -1964

Chronology-Documents-Bibliographical Aids

Edited by
Arnold S. Rice

Series Editor
Howard F. Bremer

1971
OCEANA PUBLICATIONS, INC.
Dobbs Ferry, New York

Library of Congress Catalog Card Number: 78-111215
International Standard Book Number: 0-379-12071-2

Manufactured in the United States of America

CONTENTS

CONTENTS

EDITOR'S FOREWORD

The purpose of this undertaking is to provide in a single volume to one interested in the life and times of Herbert Clark Hoover the following: (1) the pertinent facts relating to the man from his birth to his death--arranged chronologically; (2) the key documents of his Presidency; (3) a comprehensive bibliography of both the primary sources and secondary works.

The greatest care has been exercised to list accurately the year, month, and day for each entry in the Chronology. For some events in the early period of Hoover's life the precise dates have not been successfully traced because documentation is either lacking or conflicting. Where this is the case, therefore, only the year and month are given in the entry.

Having a book published is an important occurrence in life. Hoover produced thirty-three works. Since he was so prolific in this aspect of his career, it was decided because of limitations of space not to indicate in the Chronology the appearance of each volume. However, in the Bibliographical Aids section a separate category is devoted to the most significant works by Hoover, with, of course, the date of publication for each.

CHRONOLOGY

CHRONOLOGY

YOUTH AND PROFESSIONAL CAREER

1874

August 10   Was born in West Branch, Iowa, to Jesse Hoover, a blacksmith and dealer in farm implements, and Hulda Minthorn Hoover, a teacher.

1876

September 1   His only sister, May, was born in West Branch, Iowa. (His only brother, Theodore, had been born on January 28, 1871, in West Branch, Iowa.)

1879

September 1   Enrolled in a public elementary school in West Branch, Iowa.

1880

December 10   His father died of typhoid fever at the age of 34 in West Branch, Iowa.

1883

February 24   His mother died of pneumonia at the age of 34 in West Branch, Iowa.

March   Went to live on the farm of a paternal uncle, Allan Hoover, near West Branch, Iowa, while his brother was taken in by another paternal uncle and his sister by the maternal grandmother.

1884

September   Went to live in Newberg, Oregon, at the home of a maternal uncle, Dr. Henry J. Minthorn, a physician. Hoover enrolled at the Friends' Pacific Academy, a Quaker school which Dr. Minthorn had helped to found and conduct.

1

1888

September   Moved, with the Minthorn family, to Salem, Oregon.
                 Employed by a land-settlement business founded by
                 Dr. Minthorn, Hoover served as office boy, an as-
                 signment which was to last 2 years.

1891

October 1   Enrolled at Leland Stanford Junior University in Palo
                 Alto, California, where he majored in geology.

1892

June-August   Served as an assistant on the Arkansas State Geo-
                 logical Survey team.

1893

June-August   Served on the United States Geological Survey team
                 in California.

1894

June-August   Served on the United States Geological Survey team
                 in Nevada.

1895

May 26   Graduated from Stanford University with an A.B.
                 degree.

June-   Employed by the Reward Mine in Nevada City, Cali-
September   fornia, first as a cart operator and then as a driller.

1896

February-   Employed by the mining engineer Louis Janin, of San
December   Francisco, for whom he worked on assignments in
                 the states of California, Colorado, and New Mexico.

1897

February   Employed by the mining firm of Bewick, Moreing and
                 Company, of London, for which he went to western
                 Australia to manage one of its gold mines, an assign-
                 ment which was to last 2 years.

1899

February 10   Married Lou Henry in Monterey, California. (She had been born on March 29, 1875, in Waterloo, Iowa, to Charles Henry, a banker, and Florence Weed Henry. She had first met Hoover in her freshman year at Stanford University, where she majored in geology and from which she graduated in 1898 with an A.B. degree.)

February 11   Sailed with his bride from the United States to China, from whose government he had accepted an offer to oversee a program of developing its natural resources, an assignment which was to last 3 years.

1900

June 10-   Participated in the defense of Tientsin, China, until
July 14   the arrival of an international relief expedition, during the Boxer Rebellion, the anti-foreign uprising in China.

1901

November 4   Made a partner in Bewick, Moreing and Company. During the next 7 years his business trips as a mining engineer were to take him, most of the time accompanied by his wife, to many parts of the world.

1903

August 4   His first child, Herbert Clark Jr., was born in London.

1907

July 17   His second child, Allan Henry, was born in London.

1908

July 22   Resigned from Bewick, Moreing and Company, and then started a consulting mining engineering firm with offices in New York City, San Francisco, and London, and later in Petrograd (now Leningrad) and Paris. Within 6 years his wealth was to total approximately $4 million. During this period his business trips were to take him, most of the time accompanied by his wife, to many parts of the world.

EARLY GOVERNMENT SERVICE

1914

August 3
Upon the request of the American ambassador to Great Britain, Walter Hines Page, Hoover, then in London on business, organized and subsequently directed the American Relief Committee, which helped 120,000 Americans stranded in Europe by the start of World War I to return to the United States.

November 5
Upon the request of the Belgian, French, and American ambassadors to Great Britain, Hoover, then in London on business, organized and subsequently directed a program for the relief of 10 million Belgians and Frenchmen whose lands had been invaded by the German army. The Commission for Relief in Belgium financed more than $1 billion worth of imports. When the United States entered World War I on April 6, 1917, he handed over the relief operation to neutral Spain and the Netherlands and returned to the United States.

1917

August 10
Appointed Food Administrator by President Woodrow Wilson. The Lever Food and Fuel Control Act gave the Food Administration authorization to control production, cut waste, and fix prices of American food during World War I.

September 1
The Grain Corporation of the Food Administration began its operation of buying, storing, and selling grain, fixing the price of wheat, and prohibiting the use of food products in the manufacture of distilled beverages.

1918

January 26
Requested, as Food Administrator, a voluntary observance of wheatless Mondays and Wednesdays, meatless Tuesdays, porkless Thursdays and Saturdays, and the use of "Victory Bread," which contained more of the wheat germ than ordinary white bread did.

July 1   The Sugar Equalization Board of the Food Administration effected a sugar rationing system, limiting each person to 2 pounds a month.

November 2   Wrote a letter, soon made public, urging the voters to choose in the Congressional elections senators and representatives, irrespective of political party, who would support President Wilson in his wartime role.

November 16   Sailed from the United States to Europe to set up headquarters in Paris for the establishment and administration of a program of postwar European food relief.

1919

March 2   Appointed Director General of the American Relief Administration by President Wilson. During its 4 months of existence, the agency delivered more than 23 million tons of food to 23 European nations with a total population of more than 300 million.

July 7   Transformed, with aid from colleagues in the Food Administration, the public American Relief Administration into a private organization to continue the work of European food relief.

September 13   Returned to the United States. For the next 1 1/2 years he had an office at 42 Broadway in New York City and kept apartments for himself and his family in New York City and Washington, D.C. During this period he wrote 28 magazine articles, delivered 46 addresses, presided over 15 public meetings, and testified at 9 Congressional hearings.

October 2   Delivered an address at Stanford University, supporting the League of Nations concept and urging the ratification of the Treaty of Versailles by the Senate.

October 14   Led the official reception in San Francisco in honor of King Albert, Queen Elizabeth, and Crown Prince Leopold of Belgium, who were making a goodwill visit to the United States.

October 15   Delivered an address in San Francisco, asserting that the achievement of permanent peace lay in sustaining the new representative governments in Europe.

November 19   Sent a letter to President Wilson urging him to accept reservations to the League of Nations document in order to secure its acceptance by the Senate. Upon the request of Democratic Senator Gilbert M. Hitchcock of Nebraska, acting minority leader of the Upper House, the text of the letter was sent to each member of the Senate Committee on Foreign Relations.

December 1   Served as chairman of a conference in Washington, D.C., called by President Wilson to study the growing conflict between management and labor. The conference ended its work with a series of recommendations published in March, 1920.

1920

February 9   Issued a statement requesting those who were working on his behalf for the Presidential nomination by the Republican Party to cease their efforts.

February 23   Delivered an address at Johns Hopkins University at Baltimore, urging first that President Wilson accept reservations to the League of Nations document and then that the Senate ratify the Treaty of Versailles, which incorporated the League.

June 11   His name was placed in nomination for President at the Republican Party National Convention at the Coliseum in Chicago. Senator Warren G. Harding of Ohio was nominated for President and Governor Calvin Coolidge of Massachusetts was nominated for Vice President.

September 6   Delivered an address at the United States Military Academy in West Point, New York, praising the initial work of the League of Nations.

September 27 — Appointed chairman of the European Relief Council, which was comprised of a variety of organizations engaged in European relief work, such as the American Red Cross, the Friends Service Committee, the Federal Council of Churches, the Knights of Columbus, and the Jewish Joint Distribution Committee.

October 9 — Addressed a Republican Party meeting in Indianapolis, urging the United States to join the League of Nations, with reservations if necessary.

October 11 — Addressed the American Child Hygiene Association in St. Louis, Missouri, advocating physical examinations in schools, free lunches in schools of certain geographic areas, and the prohibition of child labor.

October 15 — Made public was a statement signed by Hoover and 30 other prominent Republicans, including Charles Evans Hughes, Elihu Root, and Henry L. Stimson, announcing their belief that if the Republican Party candidate for President were elected he would take the United States into the League of Nations with reservations.

November 19 — Elected president of the American Engineering Council, a body of the leading engineering societies designed to give members of the profession an outlet for their collective views on public issues.

December 10 — Addressed a committee of the American Bankers Association in Chicago, advocating that American credit extended to the European nations in the postwar period be private rather than governmental.

1921

January 10 — Bought, at 2300 S Street in Washington, D.C., a home which was to serve Hoover and his family until he occupied the White House.

January 27   Rejected an offer of a partnership in the Guggenheim-
                    controlled American Smelting and Refining Company,
                    the world's largest mining and metallurgical firm, in
                    favor of the imminent tender of a Cabinet appointment.

SECRETARY OF COMMERCE AND BEYOND

March 3   Appointed Secretary of Commerce by President Hard-
                    ing. Hoover continued serving in the post through the
                    Coolidge Administration until July, 1928.

March 19   Invited 25 leaders in business, labor, and agriculture
                    to serve on an advisory committee dealing with the
                    policies and programs of the Dept. of Commerce.

September 26   Served as chairman of the Unemployment Conference
                    in Washington, D.C., called by President Harding.
                    The number of enemployed throughout the nation was
                    approximately 3.5 million.

1922
February 27   Upon the call of Hoover, the first national radio con-
                    ference was held in Washington, D.C., to consider
                    the regulation of broadcasting. It was attended by
                    government officials, representatives of the radio
                    industry, and radio amateurs. To sustain this co-
                    operative action Hoover called a similar conference
                    for each of the next 3 years.

May 18   Presented the case against the 12-hour work day and
                    the 84-hour work week in the steel industry at a con-
                    ference of steel manufacturers at the White House
                    called by President Harding.

1923
July 3   Joined, in Tacoma, Washington, the official party of
                    President Harding's visit to Canada and Alaska. Dur-
                    ing the trip Harding sought Hoover's advice on the ex-
                    posure of corruption in the Administration. On the
                    return, Harding died in San Francisco on August 2.

July 20   Received a scroll from the Soviet Union thanking him for his efforts, as chairman of the American Relief Administration, in helping to alleviate the famine in the Ukraine and in the Volga River Valley from the fall of 1921 to the spring of 1923.

1924

March 14   Appointed by President Coolidge chairman of the American St. Lawrence Commission, which was to cooperate with a like commission of the Canadian government on the development of the St. Lawrence River and Great Lakes Systems.

September 5   Addressed the annual convention of the United States Fisheries Association in Atlantic City, summarizing the work the government had done in protecting American fisheries.

1925

June 25   His son, Herbert, Jr., married Margaret E. Watson in Palo Alto, California.

September 23   Sent a memorandum to the President's Aircraft Board recommending the establishment of a Bureau of Civil Aviation through which the federal government would render services to commercial aviation comparable to those which it had given for over a century to commercial navigation. The Congress enacted the recommendation in May, 1926.

June 27   Delivered addresses in Sacramento and Stockton, California, advising that the state of California and the federal government establish a joint commission to develop the Sacramento and San Joaquin Valleys.

1926

August 21   Delivered addresses in Tacoma and Seattle, Washington, advising that the state of Washington and the federal government establish a joint commission to develop the Columbia River Basin.

1927

April 7   In his capacity as Secretary of Commerce, Hoover
               in Washington, D.C., was seen and heard by a group
               at the Bell Telephone Laboratories in New York City,
               in the first demonstration of a telecast transmitted
               over a considerable distance.

July 20   Prompted by the spring flooding of the lower Missis-
               sippi River Valley, causing a property loss of $300
               million, Hoover submitted a report to President Cool-
               idge emphasizing the need of completely revising
               the federal government flood control program.

August 2   President Coolidge issued the statement: "I do not
               choose to run for President in nineteen-twenty-eight."
               Hoover was immediately urged by political associates
               to announce his candidacy for President.

October 4   Served as chairman of the first international radio
               conference, in Washington, D.C., to consider the
               international regulation of broadcasting. It was at-
               tended by delegates from 76 nations.

1928

February 12   Formally announced his candidacy for President by
               permitting his name to be entered in the Republican
               Party primary in Ohio.

June 14   Nominated for President on the first ballot at the Re-
               publican Party National Convention at the Civic Audi-
               torium in Kansas City, Missouri. Senator Charles
               Curtis of Kansas was nominated for Vice President.

June 28   Governor Alfred E. Smith of New York was nominated
               for President on the first ballot at the Democratic
               Party National Convention at Sam Houston Hall in
               Houston, Texas. Senator Joseph T. Robinson of Ar-
               kansas was nominated for Vice President.

July 14   Completed his last day of work as Secretary of Commerce, after having submitted his resignation from the post.

August 11   Formally accepted, in Palo Alto, California, the nomination for President by the Republican Party.

August 21   Delivered a campaign speech in West Branch, Iowa, on farm relief and the development of inland waterway systems.

September 17   Delivered a campaign speech in Newark, New Jersey, on unemployment.

October 6   Delivered a campaign speech in Elizabethton, Tennessee, on the way in which the federal government could assist Southern progress.

October 15   Delivered a campaign speech in Boston on international trade and tariffs.

October 22   Delivered a campaign speech in New York City on his philosophy of "rugged individualism."

November 6   Elected President of the United States. He carried 40 states to Smith's 8; his popular vote was 21,392,190 to Smith's 15,016,443; in the Electoral College he won 444 votes to Smith's 87.

November 19   Sailed with his wife on the battleship Maryland from the United States to Latin America to take a goodwill tour. He returned on the battleship Utah to the United States on January 6, 1929.

December 17   Under Secretary of State J. Reuben Clark drafted a memorandum declaring that the United States would not again claim the right to intervene in the internal affairs of a Latin American nation as an "international policeman," in effect repudiating the Roosevelt Corollary to the Monroe Doctrine. The Hoover Administration published the memorandum in March, 1930.

December 21   Congress passed the Boulder Dam Project Bill com-
                   mitting the federal government to participation in the
                   production of hydroelectric power.

PRESIDENT

1929

March 4   Inaugurated as 31st President of the United States in
                   Washington, D.C. At 1:08 p.m. Chief Justice William
                   H. Taft administered the oath of office.

March 5   Held his first press conference at the White House,
                   during which he outlined what he believed should be
                   the relationship of the President and the press to each
                   other.

March 12   Declared at a press conference that there would be
                   no leases or disposal of federal government oil lands,
                   except for those made mandatory by acts of Congress.

March 22   Issued a Presidential Proclamation announcing that
                   the "national origins" clause of the Immigration Act
                   of 1924 would go into effect on July 1, 1929. Accord-
                   ing to this clause, the total number of immigrants
                   from European quota countries was restricted to
                   153,774 annually. Each country was given a quota
                   based on the percentage of that national origin in the
                   American population in 1920.

April 15   Upon the call of Hoover, Congress convened in special
                   session to deal with farm relief and limited revision
                   of the tariff. The Senate passed the Export Debenture
                   Plan Bill by which the federal government would pay
                   a farmer a subsidy for exporting his surplus crop;
                   the House of Representatives, however, rejected the
                   measure.

May 28   Announced the appointment of the National Commis-
                sion on Law Observance and Enforcement, with for-
                mer Attorney General George W. Wickersham as
                chairman, to conduct an investigation of prohibition
                and related problems of law enforcement. It was
                soon to be familiarly known as the Wickersham Com-
                mission.

June 7   A committee of the Allied Powers of World War I in
                Paris announced that the Owen D. Young Plan would
                supersede the Charles G. Dawes Plan of August 16,
                1924, for the payment of German reparations.

June 15   Upon the recommendation of Hoover, Congress passed
                the Agricultural Marketing Bill establishing a Fed-
                eral Farm Board to promote the marketing of farm
                products through the extension of loans to agricultural
                cooperatives.

July 24   Proclaimed in effect the Kellogg-Briand Pact outlaw-
                ing war as an instrument of national policy. Devel-
                oping from negotiations between the American Sec-
                retary of State Frank B. Kellogg and the French For-
                eign Minister Aristide Briand, the Pact was signed
                by 15 nations in Paris on August 27, 1928, and was
                eventually to have a total of 62 nations as signatories.

October 4   Upon the invitation of Hoover, Prime Minister J.
                Ramsay MacDonald of Great Britain arrived in Wash-
                ington, D.C., to confer on naval parity. Hoover ac-
                cepted the suggestion to hold a multinational naval
                disarmament conference in London in January, 1930.

October 10   Issued a joint statement with Prime Minister Mac-
                Donald reaffirming American and British support of
                the Kellogg-Briand Pact.

October 21   Delivered an address in Dearborn, Michigan, at the
                celebration of the 50th anniversary of the invention
                of the electric incandescent lamp by Thomas A.
                Edison.

October 24   The New York stock market collapsed. Over 13 mil-
                  lion shares were traded on the New York Stock Ex-
                  change on this day, soon to be known as "Black Thurs-
                  day." Over 16 million shares were traded on October
                  29. By November 14 approximately $30 billion in the
                  market value of listed stocks had been wiped out.

November 21   Conferred privately at the White House first with
                  industrialists and then with labor leaders on the eco-
                  nomic crisis.

November 29   Rear Admiral Richard E. Byrd and his pilot became
                  the first men to fly over the South Pole.

December 2   Secretary of State Henry L. Stimson sent identical
                  notes to the Soviet Union and China appealing to them,
                  as signers of the Kellogg-Briand Pact, to settle ami-
                  cably their dispute in Manchuria.

December 3   Delivered his first Annual Message to Congress, de-
                  claring his belief that business confidence had been
                  re-established in the nation since the New York stock
                  market crash on October 24, 1929.

December 4   Transmitted to Congress the budget of the United
                  States for the fiscal year ending June 30, 1931.

December 9   The American chargé d'affaires in Berne, Switzer-
                  land, signed the Elihu Root formula, as a basis for
                  the adherence of the United States to the World Court.
                  This was accepted by Secretary of State Stimson.

                                    1930
January 1   Held the traditional New Year's Day reception at the
                  White House, shaking hands with some 9,000 people.
                  Considering this an unnecessary ordeal, he managed
                  to avoid future New Year's Day receptions as Presi-
                  dent by being away from Washington, D.C., on the
                  first day of the year.

January 2   Started a week-long series of conferences with Congressional leaders on the use of an extensive public works program to help deal with the economic crisis.

February 3   Appointed former Secretary of State Charles Evans Hughes Chief Justice of the Supreme Court.

March 8   Issued a Presidential Proclamation announcing the death of William H. Taft and ordering a period of public mourning.

April 10   Nominated John J. Parker, a judge of the United States Court of Appeals for the Fourth Circuit, to be an Associate Justice of the Supreme Court. Negro organizations and labor unions opposed the jurist because of his views, and the Senate refused to confirm the nomination.

April 14   Addressed the annual convention of the Daughters of the American Revolution in Washington, D.C., on the duty of the United States to promote world peace.

April 22   The London Naval Treaty, among other things, limiting submarine, cruiser, and destroyer construction, was signed by the United States, Great Britain, and Japan. The London Naval Conference had begun its deliberations on January 21, 1930, with France and Italy joining the United States, Great Britain, and Japan. Eventually France and Italy withdrew from the conference, leaving the remaining nations to sign the treaty.

May 20   Appointed Owen J. Roberts, the government prosecutor in the Teapot Dome oil scandal case, an Associate Justice of the Supreme Court.

May 28   Vetoed the Spanish War Veterans Pension Bill; the Congress overrode the veto on June 2.

June 17   Signed the Hawley-Smoot Tariff Bill providing for the
                   highest tariff rates in the history of the nation. Hoover
                   had received a petition signed by 1,028 economists,
                   urging a Presidential veto of the protective tariff bill
                   if it were passed by Congress.

August 14   Conferred with the governors of various Midwestern
                   and Southern states on the extensive drought that was
                   affecting their region.

September 17   Boulder Dam (later to be renamed Hoover Dam), near
                   Las Vegas, Nevada, was dedicated and construction
                   begun. The project was completed in 1936.

                   Former Secretary of State Kellogg was elected a
                   member of the World Court by the League of Nations.

October 2   Addressed the annual convention of the American
                   Bankers Association in Cleveland, on what he believed
                   to be the causes of the Depression and the way in
                   which bankers could contribute to ending the economic
                   crisis.

November 4   In the mid-term Congressional elections the Demo-
                   cratic Party gained 8 seats in the Senate and 53 in the
                   House of Representatives, securing for the Demo-
                   cratic Party a majority in the Lower House.

November 19   Upon the call of Hoover, the White House Conference
                   on Child Health and Protection began its deliberations.

December 2   Delivered his second Annual Message to Congress,
                   requesting an appropriation of from $100 million to
                   $150 million for the construction of public works to
                   reduce unemployment.

December 3   Transmitted to Congress the budget of the United
                   States for the fiscal year ending June 30, 1932.

December 10   Submitted to the Senate the Elihu Root formula for the adherence of the United States to the World Court. The Senate failed to deliberate the matter.

December 20   Congress authorized the expenditure of $116 million for the construction of public works.

Congress passed the Drought Relief Bill authorizing the expenditure of $45 million.

1931

January 7   Colonel Arthur Woods, chairman of the President's Emergency Committee for Unemployment Relief, issued a report that the national unemployment figure was between 4 million and 5 million.

January 20   Submitted to Congress the report of the Wickersham Commission, which declared that prohibition was not being effectively enforced.

February 6   Secretary of State Stimson as a goodwill gesture announced that the United States would abandon the use of moral standards, as first evolved by President Wilson, as a test for the diplomatic recognition of new governments in Latin America.

February 12   Delivered a radio address from the White House warning of the dangers to individual freedom and initiative if the federal government assumed the responsibility for local emergency relief.

February 26   Vetoed the Soldiers' Bonus Loan Bill extending cash loans to veterans up to 50 percent of their adjusted compensation certificates; the Congress overrode the veto on the following day.

February 27   Issued an Executive Order placing the government of the Virgin Islands under the supervision of the Department of the Interior.

March 3   .   Signed a bill which designated "The Star-Spangled Banner" as the national anthem.

Vetoed the bill of Republican Senator George Norris of Nebraska for a federal public works project at Muscle Shoals on the Tennessee River, on the ground that the government operation would compete with private enterprise.

April 14   Delivered a radio address from Washington, D.C., in celebration of the 50th anniversary of the founding of Tuskegee Institute, citing the contribution of Tuskegee to the progress of black Americans.

April 29   Received the first absolute monarch to visit the United States, King Prajadhipok of Siam.

May 1   The Empire State Building, the tallest skyscraper in the world, was dedicated in New York City.

May 4   Addressed the annual convention of the international Chamber of Commerce in Washington, D.C., urging the reduction of armaments as being essential to world peace and prosperity.

May 30   Delivered a Memorial Day Address at Valley Forge, Pennsylvania, declaring that the American people were at the time experiencing the "Valley Forge" of the Depression.

June 16   Delivered an address at the dedication of the Harding Memorial in Marion, Ohio, treating both the service rendered to the nation by Harding and the tragedy that beset his Administration.

June 20   Proposed a year's moratorium on all intergovernment debts and reparations. This was accepted in principle by each of the important creditor nations by the following July 6, and was soon put into operation by creditor and debtor nations agreeable to the proposal.

September 18   Japanese troops marched into Manchuria, violating the Kellogg-Briand Pact.

September 21   Addressed the annual convention of the American Legion in Detroit, declaring that to oppose any additional government expenditures was to perform a patriotic service.

October 16   The League of Nations invited the United States to send a representative to participate in its deliberations on Japan's invasion of Manchuria. Secretary of State Stimson appointed Prentiss B. Gilbert, United States Consul General at Geneva, Switzerland, to serve. Hoover announced that he would cooperate with the League of Nations in this matter, although he was opposed to the currently discussed use of economic sanctions against Japan.

Proposed at a press conference drastic economies in public expenditures, with special reference to the naval budget.

October 17   Al Capone was found guilty of income tax evasion and sentenced to 11 years' imprisonment and a $50,000 fine.

October 18   Delivered a radio address from Fortress Monroe, Virginia, appealing for voluntary local relief of the unemployed.

October 24   The George Washington Bridge spanning the Hudson River was formally opened.

October 25   Issued a joint statement with Premier Pierre Laval of France after conferring in Washington, D.C., agreeing to continue the gold standard in the United States and France. Great Britain had abandoned the gold standard the preceding month.

October 27   Opposed, in a press statement, the independence of
                  the Philippines until economic stability was achieved
                  in the islands.

November 6   Announced a reduction in federal departmental budg-
                  ets, and declared further that a "sound" fiscal posi-
                  tion of the government was necessary for the return
                  of national prosperity.

December 7   "Hunger marchers," with a petition for a guarantee
                  of employment at a minimum wage, were denied ad-
                  mission to the White House.

December 8   Delivered his third Annual Message to Congress,
                  recommending the establishment of an emergency
                  reconstruction finance corporation and a system of
                  federal home loan banks.

December 9   Transmitted to Congress the budget of the United
                  States for the fiscal year ending June 30, 1933.

December 10   The League of Nations appointed the British Earl of
                  Lytton chairman of a commission to investigate Japan's
                  invasion of Manchuria. The Lytton Commission in-
                  cluded Major General Frank R. McCoy as the Amer-
                  ican representative.

December 12   Submitted to the Senate for the second time the Elihu
                  Root formula for the adherence of the United States
                  to the World Court. The Senate again failed to de-
                  liberate the matter.

                                        1932
January 7   Secretary of State Stimson sent identical notes to
                  Japan and China, as a result of the former's occupa-
                  tion of Manchuria, declaring that the United States
                  would not recognize any treaty or agreement impair-
                  ing the political independence or territorial integrity
                  of China. This declaration of nonrecognition was
                  soon to be familiarly known as the Stimson Doctrine.

January 8	Declared at a press conference that economy in government expenditures was necessary for national economic recovery.
January 22	Signed the bill establishing the Reconstruction Finance Corporation to provide federal government loans to banks, railroads, and insurance companies. Hoover appointed former Vice President Charles G. Dawes chairman of the RFC, which lent $1.2 billion during its initial 6 months of operation.
January 29	Japanese army and naval forces attacked and invaded Shanghai, China, prompting an official protest from the United States.
February 2	The World Disarmament Conference began its deliberations in Geneva, Switzerland, under the auspices of the League of Nations. Sixty nations, including the United States, participated, but with little result.
February 3	Appealed to the American people to resist the then common practice of hoarding money, as he believed it hindered national economic recovery.
February 5	Appointed Secretary of the Treasury Andrew W. Mellon ambassador to Great Britain.
February 10	Secretary of War Patrick J. Hurley, as a result of a tour of investigation, reported that the Philippines was not yet ready for independence.
February 17	Submitted a message to Congress urging a general reorganization of government departments and a consolidation of lesser government bureaus as economy measures.
February 22	Addressed a joint session of Congress, formally observing the bicentennial anniversary of the birth of George Washington.

February 27   Signed the Glass-Steagall Bill facilitating the redis-
               counting of commercial paper by the federal reserve
               banks and making $750 million in government gold
               available for business loans.

March 1   The 1 1/2-year-old son of Charles A. Lindbergh was
               kidnapped near Hopewell, New Jersey.

March 2   Appointed Benjamin N. Cardozo, Chief Justice of the
               New York Court of Appeals, an Associate Justice of
               the Supreme Court.

March 7   Congress authorized the distribution of 40 million
               bushels of wheat of the Federal Farm Board through
               the agency of the American Red Cross. An additional
               45 million bushels was authorized on the following
               July 5.

March 23   Signed the Norris-La Guardia Bill forbidding the use
               of injunctions to prevent strikes, picketing, and boy-
               cotts.

March 25   Declared at a press conference that balancing the
               budget was necessary for national economic recovery.

March 29   Declared his opposition to bonus legislation as undoing
               the effort of his Administration to balance the budget.

April 4   Submitted a message to Congress emphasizing the
               need for legislation to help balance the budget.

May 22   Norman M. Thomas of New York was nominated for
               President at the Socialist Party National Convention
               in Milwaukee, Wisconsin. James H. Maurer of Penn-
               sylvania was nominated for Vice President.

May 28   William Z. Foster of New York was nominated for
               President at the Communist Party National Convention
               in Chicago. James W. Ford of New York was nomi-
               nated for Vice President.

May 31   Addressed the Senate, stressing the need for a balanced budget.

June 10   Delivered an address at the commencement exercises of Howard University in Washington, D.C., on the importance of preparing blacks to become leaders of their race.

June 16   Nominated for President on the first ballot at the Republican Party National Convention at the Chicago Stadium in Chicago. Vice President Curtis was renominated for that office.

June 17   The Senate rejected the Patman Bonus Bill, which the House of Representatives had passed, providing for the payment of the balance of the bonus certificates of World War I veterans with paper money. Hoover had opposed the bill as being inflationary.

June 21   Presented the National Geographic Society special gold medal at Constitution Hall in Washington, D.C., to Amelia Earhart, for having become on May 21, 1932, the first woman to achieve a solo transatlantic flight.

July 1   Governor Franklin D. Roosevelt of New York was nominated for President on the fourth ballot at the Democratic Party National Convention at the Chicago Stadium in Chicago. Speaker of the House of Representatives John N. Garner of Texas was nominated for Vice President.

July 7   William D. Upshaw of Georgia was nominated for President at the Prohibition Party National Convention in Indianapolis, Indiana. Frank S. Regan of Illinois was nominated for Vice President.

July 9   A conference of European nations in Lausanne, Switzerland, ended its 3 weeks of deliberations, agreeing to the virtual cancellation of German reparations if an equivalent cancellation of their war debts to the United States could be arranged. Hoover opposed the plan of the Lausanne Conference.

July 11   Vetoed the Wagner-Garner Bill extending the work of federal employment agencies to states which did not sponsor their own employment units, on the ground that it would interfere with state control over unemployment relief.

July 18   Representatives of the United States and Canada signed the St. Lawrence Deep-Waterway Treaty to build a Great Lakes-St. Lawrence seaway, but the Senate refused to ratify the treaty.

July 21   Signed the Relief and Construction Bill enabling the Reconstruction Finance Corporation to lend $1.8 billion to states for their relief programs and their public works.

July 22   Signed the Federal Home Loan Bank Bill establishing 8 to 12 home loan banks in different sections of the nation to make loans to mortgage-lending institutions, in order to stimulate the construction of private dwellings and thus increase employment.

July 28   Ordered federal troops, under General Douglas A. MacArthur, to drive the last of the "Bonus Army" out of Washington, D.C. Some 1,000 World War I veterans had descended on the national capital on the preceding May 29, declaring that they would remain there until Congress authorized the cash payment of the balance of their bonus certificates. Other veterans arrived in the city, bringing the total number to over 15,000 by mid-June. By mid-July most of them had departed but some 2,000 had refused to disband. The removal of the rest of the "Bonus Army" was completed with the use of the infantry, cavalry, and tank corps on July 29.

August 11   Formally accepted the nomination for President by the Republican Party at Constitution Hall in Washington, D.C.

August 26   The Controller of the Currency ordered a moratorium on first-mortgage foreclosures.

October 1   Addressed the Republican Party Joint National Planning Committee in Washington, D.C., pledging the Administration's protection of the rights of Negroes and emphasizing the importance to the Republican Party of the black vote.

October 4   Delivered a major campaign speech in Des Moines, Iowa, on agriculture.

                 The Lytton Commission published its report on the Manchurian crisis, condemning Japan but also proposing that Manchuria become an autonomous state under Chinese sovereignty but Japanese control. The League of Nations adopted the report on February 24, 1933, and Japan gave notice of its withdrawal from the organization on March 27, 1933.

October 5   Delivered train-stop campaign remarks in Fort Wayne, Indiana, rebutting Democratic Party charges of his insensitivity to the economic plight of the American people.

October 15   Delivered train-stop campaign remarks in Cumberland, Maryland, on the protective tariff.

                 Delivered a major campaign speech in Cleveland on unemployment.

October 22   Delivered a campaign speech in Charleston, West Virginia, emphasizing the importance of the protective tariff to the state of West Virginia.

Delivered a major campaign speech in Detroit, attacking the statements of Democratic Party Presidential candidate Roosevelt regarding government finances.

October 28   Delivered a major campaign speech in Indianapolis, comparing the Administration's domestic policies with those advocated by the Democratic Party.

October 31   Delivered a major campaign speech at Madison Square Garden in New York City, analyzing the Democratic Party philosophy of government as being dangerous to the foundations of American national life.

November 4   Delivered a major campaign speech in St. Louis, characterizing the Democratic Party campaign as one that avoided dealing with specific issues.

November 5   Delivered a major campaign speech in St. Paul, Minnesota, contrasting the Administration's measures to accomplish economic recovery with those advocated by the Democratic Party candidates.

November 7   Delivered a major campaign speech in Salt Lake City, reviewing Republican Party policies on a variety of domestic and foreign issues.

Delivered a radio campaign speech from Elko, Nevada, declaring that the election results would affect the welfare of generations of Americans to come.

In Powell v. Alabama the Supreme Court granted a retrial for the 9 black youths of the Scottsboro case, declaring that the defendants, who were found guilty of rape by an Alabama court in 1931, had not been properly represented by counsel at their initial trial.

November 8   Was defeated for President. He carried 6 states to Roosevelt's 42; his popular vote was 15,761,841 to Roosevelt's 22,821,857; in the Electoral College he won 59 votes to Roosevelt's 472.

November 11   The Tomb of the Unknown Soldier in Arlington National Cemetery was dedicated by Secretary of War Patrick J. Hurley.

November 12   Delivered an address in Glendale, California, appealing to Republicans to cooperate with the Roosevelt Administration in its attempts to end the Depression.

November 22   Upon the invitation of Hoover, President-elect Roosevelt called at the White House to confer on Great Britain's request for the suspension of payments of her war debt to the United States.

December 6   Delivered his fourth Annual Message to Congress, recommending the reorganization of the American banking system, the passage of an excise tax, a reorganization of the government through the restructuring of the executive and independent agencies, a reduction of government expenditures, and the balancing of the budget.

December 7   Transmitted to Congress the budget of the United States for the fiscal year ending June 30, 1934.

December 10   Addressed the Gridiron Club in Washington, D.C., stressing the need for the 2-party system, but also for Republican cooperation with the Roosevelt Administration.

December 15   Delivered an address at the laying of the cornerstone of the new Department of Labor Building in Washington, D.C., extolling labor's role in the American past.

               Of 11 debtor nations to the United States, 5, including France, defaulted in their payments.

                              1933
January 2   The last American marines were withdrawn from Nicaragua, ending a 20-year occupation by the United States.

January 5   Issued a Presidential Proclamation announcing the
                 death of Calvin Coolidge and ordering a period of
                 public mourning.

January 11   Submitted a message to Congress recommending the
                 immediate passage of legislation to revise the bank-
                 ruptcy laws for the relief of debtors.

January 13   Vetoed the Hawes-Cutting Bill granting the Philippines
                 independence after a 10-year period of protectorate
                 status; the Congress overrode the veto on January 17.
                 The act, however, was never to go into effect, as it
                 did not receive approval from the Philippines itself.

January 17   Sent a message to Congress declaring the urgent ne-
                 cessity of balancing the budget by reducing expendi-
                 tures and increasing revenues. A sales tax was rec-
                 ommended as a solution.

January 20   Conferred with President-elect Roosevelt at the White
                 House on a variety of domestic and foreign issues,
                 with emphasis on the subject of European war debts
                 to the United States.

January 23   The 20th ("Lame Duck") Amendment to the Constitu-
                 tion was ratified. According to the Amendment, Con-
                 gress is to convene each year on January 3 and the
                 terms of the President and Vice President are to be-
                 gin on the January 20 following the national election.

February 13   Addressed the National Republican Club in New York
                 City, urging international cooperation to restore
                 worldwide economic recovery, with a return to the
                 gold standard as a primary step.

February 15   President-elect Roosevelt escaped in Miami an as-
                 sassin's bullet, which mortally wounded Mayor Anton
                 J. Cermak of Chicago.

February 20   Delivered an address at the laying of the cornerstone
                 of the National Archives Building in Washington, D.C.,
                 declaring that the structure would house the precious
                 records of an indissoluble Union.

February 23   Delivered an address at the laying of the cornerstone
                 of the new Department of Justice Building in Washing-
                 ton, D.C., declaring that law is the foundation stone
                 of an organized society.

February 24   After having voted against the Lytton Commission
                 Report, the Japanese delegation walked out of the
                 League of Nations Assembly.

March 4   Attended the inauguration of Franklin D. Roosevelt
                 as the 32nd President of the United States.

                              RETIREMENT

March 21   Arrived at his home in Palo Alto, California, after
                 traveling cross-country from Washington, D.C.

                                  1934
May 5   Announced that he would not be a candidate for Presi-
                 dent in 1936, but hoped and expected to influence the
                 reorganization of the Republican Party.

                                  1935
May 15   Assailed the National Industrial Recovery Act, ad-
                 vising the House of Representatives to abolish it.

                                  1936
June 10   Addressed the Republican Party National Convention
                 at the Municipal Auditorium in Cleveland, excoriating
                 the New Deal.

October 16   Addressed a Republican Party rally in Philadelphia,
                 charging the New Deal with juggling accounts to con-
                 ceal expenditures.

October 19   Appointed chairman of the board of directors of the Boys Clubs of America, an organization in which he had long taken an active interest.

1937

February 20   Addressed the Union League in Chicago, attacking President Roosevelt's plan for reorganizing the federal judiciary, particularly the proposal on increasing the Supreme Court membership from 9 to a maximum of 15 if justices reaching the age of 70 declined to retire.

March 17   His son, Allan Henry, married Margaret Coberly in Los Angeles.

June 11   Announced that he planned to restore his birthplace in West Branch, Iowa.

1938

February 9   Sailed from the United States to Europe to go to the scenes of his activities as chairman of the Commission for Relief in Belgium during World War I. He returned to the United States on March 29.

March 31   Addressed the Council on Foreign Relations in New York City, warning the United States to keep out of war, and also to avoid alliances with other democratic nations that were actively opposed to the fascist powers. He asserted further that a planned economy and reciprocal tariff agreements were steps that would lead to armed conflict.

April 26   Addressed the Federation of Republican Women's Clubs in Fresno, California, arguing that the American government had suffered a "moral recession" under the New Deal.

1939

May 12 Honored at the Belgian Pavilion Dinner at the New York World's Fair for his European food relief activities during the World War I period.

May 21 Addressed a group of Indiana Republican newspaper editors in Warsaw, Indiana, urging the defeat of the New Deal for the good of the nation.

1940

February 11 Addressed the Jewish Welfare Fund in Chicago, envisioning the establishment of a central African state to accomodate 10 million refugees from war-torn Europe.

May 17 Delivered a radio address supporting the Roosevelt Administration's comprehensive defense program.

June 25 Addressed the Republican Party National Convention at the Municipal Auditorium in Philadelphia, characterizing the direction being taken by the New Deal as being similar to that which had brought ruin to many nations of Europe.

1941

May 11 Delivered a radio address opposing United States entry into World War II, but favoring more military aid to Great Britain.

June 29 Delivered a radio address opposing military aid to the Soviet Union.

1942

July 12 Delivered a radio address on the possible nature of the postwar period, emphasizing the need of American preparation for the peace to come.

1943

February 8 Testified at a session of a Senate appropriations subcommittee, urging a revision of American military, agricultural, and industrial manpower policies.

1944

January 7   ， His wife died of a heart attack in New York City. She was buried in Palo Alto, California.

June 27   Addressed the Republican Party National Convention at the Chicago Stadium in Chicago, calling for a concerted drive against the New Deal.

1945

May 8   Addressed the Save the Children Federation in New York City, emphasizing the immediate need of feeding postwar European sick and emaciated children.

May 28   Conferred with President Harry S Truman on a prospective program of postwar European food relief.

1946

March 17   Flew from the United States to Europe, upon the request of President Truman, to begin a world-circling trip investigating famine conditions. While in Europe he conferred with Pope Pius XII, Prime Minister Clement Attlee of Great Britain, Queen Elizabeth and Prince Charles of Belgium, and King Gustavus V of Sweden. On April 29 he flew from Europe to Asia. While in Asia he conferred with Mohandas K. Gandhi of India, President Sergio Osmena of the Philippines, and a number of Japanese officials. He returned to the United States on May 10, and submitted his report to President Truman at the White House on May 13.

1947

February 2   Flew from the United States to Europe, upon the request of President Truman, to make a survey of that continent's postwar food problems. While there he conferred with Pope Pius XII, British Foreign Minister Ernest Bevin, and a number of West German officials. He returned to the United States on February 24, and submitted his report to President Truman at the White House on February 27.

April 30   President Truman signed a bill changing the name of
                  Boulder Dam to Hoover Dam.

July 17   Appointed chairman of the Commission on Organiza-
                  tion of the Executive Branch of the Government by
                  President Truman. Soon to be familiarly known as
                  the Hoover Commission, its purpose was to suggest
                  ways of streamlining the executive branch of the fed-
                  eral government and of economizing on its operations.
                  In accepting the chairmanship, Hoover announced that
                  it was to be his "last public service."

                              1948
June 22   Addressed the Republican Party National Convention
                  at Convention Hall in Philadelphia, outlining the re-
                  sponsibility of the Republican Party to the United States
                  and the world.

October 12   Addressed the Americas Foundation in New York City,
                  urging the nations of the Western Hemisphere to stand
                  firm against Communist infiltration.

                              1949
August 29   Became a great-grandfather upon the birth of a son,
                  Steven, to Herbert Clark Hoover III and Meredith
                  McGilvray Hoover.

June 17   The Hoover Commission ended its work, after having
                  made 275 recommendations, of which some 200 were
                  put into effect.

October 24   Elected a member of the board of directors of the
                  Waldorf-Astoria Corporation.

                              1950
January 2   Called for, along with Republican Senator Robert A.
                  Taft of Ohio, American military protection of the
                  Nationalist Chinese government on the island of For-
                  mosa (now Taiwan).

April 27   Addressed the annual convention of the American
                    Newspaper Publishers Association in New York City,
                    proposing that the United Nations be reorganized to
                    exclude the Communist bloc.

December 20   Delivered a combined radio-television address urging
                    an American foreign policy based on protecting the
                    Western Hemisphere, continuing a naval presence in
                    the Atlantic and Pacific Oceans, rearming Japan, and
                    waiting for Western Europe to show a united will to
                    fight Communism before supplying it with more finan-
                    cial aid and troops.

                                        1951
February 9   Delivered a combined radio-television address pro-
                    posing a 10-point program to insure peace for the
                    United States, based on the avoiding of land wars
                    while building air and naval power sufficient to deter
                    or repel attack.

                                        1952
January 27   Delivered a combined radio-television address ad-
                    vocating the withdrawal of American troops from
                    Europe and the reliance on a well developed air-naval
                    defense of the Western Hemisphere.

July 8   Addressed the Republican Party National Convention
                    at the International Amphitheatre in Chicago, criti-
                    cizing the Democratic Party philosophy and policy.

October 18   Delivered a combined radio-television address, upon
                    the request of Republican Party Presidential candidate
                    Dwight D. Eisenhower, defending the Republican
                    Party's recent record.

                                        1953
June 8   His sister, May, died of an undisclosed illness in
                    Los Angeles.

June 14   Delivered an address at the dedication of the Theodore
                 Roosevelt home in Oyster Bay, New York.

July 21   Visited the floor of the Senate for the first time in his
                 life, receiving a standing ovation from the members
                 of that body.

September 29   Appointed chairman of the Commission on Organiza-
                 tion of the Executive Branch of the Government by
                 President Eisenhower. Familiarly known from the
                 beginning as the Second Hoover Commission, its
                 charge was similar to that of the Hoover Commission
                 of 1947-49.

October 18   Delivered, under the auspices of the Ford Foundation,
                 a television lecture on civics to the youth of the nation.

                              1954
July 21   Honored by a joint resolution of Congress on the oc-
                 casion of his approaching 80th birthday.

October 4   Attended in Washington, D.C., the swearing-in ex-
                 ercises of his son, Herbert Clark Hoover, Jr., as
                 Under Secretary of State.

November 21   Flew from the United States to West Germany in re-
                 sponse to an invitation from that nation's govern-
                 ment to pay a visit. While there he met with Chan-
                 cellor Konrad Adenauer, was given a state dinner,
                 and received an honorary degree from Tuebingen
                 University. He returned to the United States on
                 November 27.
                              1955
February 5   His brother, Theodore, died of a cerebral hemor-
                 rhage near Santa Cruz, California.

June 30   The Second Hoover Commission ended its work with
                 a series of recommendations for budgetary savings
                 to be achieved by the curtailment of federal lending
                 and medical services.

August 10   His restored boyhood home in Newberg, Oregon, was
                   dedicated as a memorial and a museum by the Hoover
                   Foundation.

October 18   Appointed an honorary member of the Woodrow Wilson
                   Centennial Celebration Commission.

                                    1956
June 5   Dedicated a junior high school in San Francisco named
                   in his honor, bringing the number of schools in the
                   nation named for him to 39.

August 21   Addressed the Republican Party National Convention
                   at the Cow Palace in San Francisco.

                                    1957
June 20   His father's restored blacksmith shop in West Branch,
                   Iowa, was dedicated as a memorial and a museum by
                   the Hoover Foundation.

July 6   Delivered an address at the dedication of the Harry
                   S. Truman Library in Independence, Missouri.

                                    1958
January 13   Received an honorary degree from The Citadel in
                   Charleston, South Carolina, bringing the number of
                   degrees granted him to 83, 1 for each year of his life.

April 19   Underwent surgery in New York City for the removal
                   of a diseased gall bladder. He left the hospital on
                   May 3.

July 4   Delivered, as the personal representative of Presi-
                   dent Eisenhower, an address during United States
                   Day ceremonies at the Brussels World's Fair, em-
                   phasizing American hopes for the well being of the
                   peoples of the world. The following day was officially
                   observed in Belgium as Herbert Hoover Day. He re-
                   turned to the United States on July 6.

July 5   Earned the distinction, as of this date, of living longer after his term of office than any other President of the United States.

August 27   Announced that he would give to charity the annual sum awarded him under a recently enacted Presidential pension plan, adding that he had given all previous personal compensation derived from government service to public or charitable enterprises.

1959

April 14   Delivered an address at the dedication of a bell tower in memory of Senator Robert A. Taft in Washington, D.C., recalling his association with the Senator.

August 9   Gave on the eve of his 85th birthday the following advice to all those seeking longevity: "Work. Don't sit around worrying about ills and pills."

1960

February 11   His medals and other tributes that had been awarded for public service were put on display at the Tiffany & Company jewelry firm in New York City.

July 25   Addressed the Republican Party National Convention at the International Amphitheatre in Chicago, arguing the need for a revival of spiritual values to counteract a longstanding moral slump. Amid a huge demonstration by the delegates, he noted that he was making his fourth "goodbye" appearance before the Republican Party.

1961

January 20   Viewed on television in Miami the inauguration in Washington, D.C., of John F. Kennedy as the 35th President of the United States, after having been prevented by inclement weather from attending in person as an invited honored guest.

March 6   Appointed honorary chairman of the New York World's
                   Fair of 1964.

                                    1962
August 10   Dedicated at his birthplace in West Branch, Iowa, the
                   Herbert Hoover Library, the repository of his Presi-
                   dential and other papers. Among the 45,000 people
                   at the ceremony was former President Truman who
                   delivered an address.

August 28   Underwent surgery in New York City for a cancerous
                   but nonrecurring intestinal tumor. He left the hospital
                   on September 18.

September 25   Narrated on a taped television program his personal
                   memoir of President Woodrow Wilson's fight for the
                   League of Nations.

                                    1963
May 22   Attended in New York City a reception in honor of
                   Major L. Gordon Cooper, Jr., the astronaut who a
                   few days earlier had made 22 orbits of the earth.
                   (This was to be Hoover's last public appearance.)

June 14   Became severely ill with anemia, as a result of bleed-
                   ing from the gastro-intestinal tract.

November 25   Unable to attend in person because of illness, he was
                   represented by his son, Herbert Hoover, Jr., at the
                   state funeral of President John F. Kennedy in Wash-
                   ington, D.C.

                                    1964
July 13   Addressed the Republican Party National Convention
                   at the Cow Palace in San Francisco, noting that he had
                   given a farewell speech to each of the preceding 5
                   Republican Party conventions. Unable to attend in
                   person because of illness, his message was read for
                   him to the delegates.

August 10   Honored on the occasion of his 90th birthday in a
                 variety of ways, such as by Presidential Proclamation,
                 a Senate resolution, and the official observance of
                 Herbert Hoover Day in 16 states. He spent his birth-
                 day eve working on his 33rd book and viewing a base-
                 ball game on television.

October 20   Died of 2 days of massive internal hemorrhaging at
                 11:35 a.m. in New York City. Both his sons were
                 with him as he slipped into a coma in his suite at the
                 Waldorf-Astoria Hotel. President Lyndon B. Johnson
                 issued a Proclamation announcing the death and order-
                 ing a period of public mourning.

October 23-24   His body lay in state in the Capitol Rotunda in Wash-
                 ington, D.C.

October 25   Was buried on a rise overlooking the home where he
                 had been born in West Branch, Iowa. One week later
                 his wife's body, taken from Palo Alto, California,
                 was placed next to his.

DOCUMENTS

INAUGURAL ADDRESS
March 4, 1929

In this address Hoover focuses on the issues of better law enforcement, the relationship of government to business, and world peace. He delivered his remarks on a rainy and chilly afternoon on the east portico of the Capitol before some 50,000 witnesses to the inauguration ceremony.

My Countrymen:

This occasion is not alone the administration of the most sacred oath which can be assumed by an American citizen. It is a dedication and consecration under God to the highest office in service of our people. I assume this trust in the humility of knowledge that only through the guidance of Almighty Providence can I hope to discharge its ever-increasing burdens.

It is in keeping with tradition throughout our history that I should express simply and directly the opinions which I hold concerning some of the matters of present importance.

OUR PROGRESS

If we survey the situation of our Nation both at home and abroad, we find many satisfactions; we find some causes for concern. We have emerged from the losses of the Great War and the reconstruction following it with increased virility and strength. From this strength we have contributed to the recovery and progress of the world. What America has done has given renewed hope and courage to all who have faith in government by the people. In the large view, we have reached a higher degree of comfort and security than ever existed before in the history of the world. Through liberation from widespread poverty we have reached a higher degree of individual freedom than ever before. The devotion to and concern for our institutions are deep and sincere. We are steadily building a new race — a new civilization great in its own attainments. The influence and high purposes of our Nation are respected among the peoples of the world. We aspire to distinction in the world, but to a distinction based upon confidence in our sense of justice as well as our accomplishments within our own borders and in our own lives. For wise guidance in this great period of recovery the Nation is deeply indebted to Calvin Coolidge.

But all this majestic advance should not obscure the constant dangers from which self-government must be safeguarded. The strong man must at all times be alert to the attack of insidious disease.

THE FAILURE OF OUR SYSTEM OF CRIMINAL JUSTICE

The most malign of all these dangers today is disregard and diso-bedience of law. Crime is increasing. Confidence in rigid and speedy justice is decreasing. I am not prepared to believe that this indicates any decay in the moral fiber of the American people. I am not pre-pared to believe that it indicates an impotence of the Federal Govern-ment to enforce its laws.

It is only in part due to the additional burdens imposed upon our judicial system by the eighteenth amendment. The problem is much wider than that. Many influences had increasingly complicated and weakened our law enforcement organization long before the adoption of the eighteenth amendment.

To reestablish the vigor and effectiveness of law enforcement we must critically consider the entire Federal machinery of justice, the redistribution of its functions, the simplification of its procedure, the provision of additional special tribunals, the better selection of juries, and the more effective organization of our agencies of investigation and prosecution that justice may be sure and that it may be swift. While the authority of the Federal Government extends to but part of our vast system of national, State, and local justice, yet the standards which the Federal Government establishes have the most profound influence upon the whole structure.

We are fortunate in the ability and integrity of our Federal judges and attorneys. But the system which these officers are called upon to administer is in many respects ill adapted to present-day conditions. Its intricate and involved rules of procedure have become the refuge of both big and little criminals. There is a belief abroad that by invok-ing technicalities, subterfuge, and delay, the ends of justice may be thwarted by those who can pay the cost.

Reform, reorganization and strengthening of our whole judicial and enforcement system both in civil and criminal sides have been advo-cated for years by statesmen, judges, and bar associations. First steps toward that end should not longer be delayed. Rigid and expedi-tious justice is the first safeguard of freedom, the basis of all ordered liberty, the vital force of progress. It must not come to be in our Re-public that it can be defeated by the indifference of the citizen, by ex-ploitation of the delays and entanglements of the law, or by combina-tions of criminals. Justice must not fail because the agencies of en-forcement are either delinquent or inefficiently organized. To consider these evils, to find their remedy, is the most sore necessity of our times.

ENFORCEMENT OF THE EIGHTEENTH AMENDMENT

Of the undoubted abuses which have grown up under the eighteenth amendment, part are due to the causes I have just mentioned; but part are due to the failure of some States to accept their share of responsibility for concurrent enforcement and to the failure of many State and local officials to accept the obligation under their oath of office zealously to enforce the laws. With the failures from these many causes has come a dangerous expansion in the criminal elements who have found enlarged opportunities in dealing in illegal liquor.

But a large responsibility rests directly upon our citizens. There would be little traffic in illegal liquor if only criminals patronized it. We must awake to the fact that this patronage from large numbers of law-abiding citizens is supplying the rewards and stimulating crime.

I have been selected by you to execute and enforce the laws of the country. I propose to do so to the extent of my own abilities, but the measure of success that the Government shall attain will depend upon the moral support which you, as citizens, extend. The duty of citizens to support the laws of the land is coequal with the duty of their Government to enforce the laws which exist. No greater national service can be given by men and women of good will — who, I know, are not unmindful of the responsibilities of citizenship — than that they should, by their example, assist in stamping out crime and outlawry by refusing participation in and condemning all transactions with illegal liquor. Our whole system of self-government will crumble either if officials elect what laws they will enforce or citizens elect what laws they will support. The worst evil of disregard for some law is that it destroys respect for all law. For our citizens to patronize the violation of a particular law on the ground that they are opposed to it is destructive of the very basis of all that protection of life, of homes and property which they rightly claim under other laws. If citizens do not like a law, their duty as honest men and women is to discourage its violation; their right is openly to work for its repeal.

To those of criminal mind there can be no appeal but vigorous enforcement of the law. Fortunately they are but a small percentage of our people. Their activities must be stopped.

A NATIONAL INVESTIGATION

I propose to appoint a national commission for a searching investigation of the whole structure of our Federal system of jurisprudence, to include the method of enforcement of the eighteenth amendment and the causes of abuse under it. Its purpose will be to make such recommendations for reorganization of the administration of Federal laws and court procedure as may be found desirable. In the meantime it is essential that a large part of the enforcement activities be transferred from the Treasury Department to the Department of Justice as a beginning of more effective organization.

THE RELATION OF GOVERNMENT TO BUSINESS

The election has again confirmed the determination of the American people that regulation of private enterprise and not Government ownership or operation is the course rightly to be pursued in our relation to business. In recent years we have established a differentiation in the whole method of business regulation between the industries which produce and distribute commodities on the one hand and public utilities on the other. In the former, our laws insist upon effective competition; in the latter, because we substantially confer a monopoly by limiting competition, we must regulate their services and rates. The rigid enforcement of the laws applicable to both groups is the very base of equal opportunity and freedom from domination for all our people, and it is just as essential for the stability and prosperity of business itself as for the protection of the public at large. Such regulation should be extended by the Federal Government within the limitations of the Constitution and only when the individual States are without power to protect their citizens through their own authority. On the other hand, we should be fearless when the authority rests only in the Federal Government.

COOPERATION BY THE GOVERNMENT

The larger purpose of our economic thought should be to establish more firmly stability and security of business and employment and thereby remove poverty still further from our borders. Our people have in recent years developed a new found capacity for cooperation among themselves to effect high purposes in public welfare. It is an advance toward the highest conception of self-government. Self-government does not and should not imply the use of political agencies alone. Progress is born of cooperation in the community — not from governmental restraints. The Government should assist and encourage these movements of collective self-help by itself cooperating with them. Business has by cooperation made great progress in the advancement of service, in stability, in regularity of employment and in the correction of its own abuses. Such progress, however, can continue only so long as business manifests its respect for law.

There is an equally important field of cooperation by the Federal Government with the multitude of agencies, State, municipal and private, in the systematic development of those processes which directly affect public health, recreation, education, and the home. We have need further to perfect the means by which Government can be adapted to human service.

EDUCATION

Although education is primarily a responsibility of the States and local communities, and rightly so, yet the Nation as a whole is vitally concerned in its development everywhere to the highest standards and to complete universality. Self-government can succeed only through an instructed electorate. Our objective is not simply to overcome illiteracy. The Nation has marched far beyond that. The more complex the problems of the Nation become, the greater is the need for more and more advanced instruction. Moreover, as our numbers increase and as our life expands with science and invention, we must discover more and more leaders for every walk of life. We can not hope to succeed in directing this increasingly complex civilization unless we can draw all the talent of leadership from the whole people. One civilization after another has been wrecked upon the attempt to secure sufficient leadership from a single group or class. If we would prevent the growth of class distinctions and would constantly refresh our leadership with the ideals of our people, we must draw constantly from the general mass. The full opportunity for every boy and girl to rise through the selective processes of education can alone secure to us this leadership.

PUBLIC HEALTH

In public health the discoveries of science have opened a new era. Many sections of our country and many groups of our citizens suffer from diseases the eradication of which are mere matters of administration and moderate expenditure. Public health service should be as fully organized and as universally incorporated into our governmental system as is public education. The returns are a thousand fold in economic benefits, and infinitely more in reduction of suffering and promotion of human happiness.

WORLD PEACE

The United States fully accepts the profound truth that our own progress, prosperity and peace are interlocked with the progress, prosperity and peace of all humanity. The whole world is at peace. The dangers to a continuation of this peace today are largely the fear and suspicion which still haunt the world. No suspicion or fear can be rightly directed toward our country.

Those who have a true understanding of America know that we have no desire for territorial expansion, for economic or other domination of other peoples. Such purposes are repugnant to our ideals of human freedom. Our form of government is ill adapted to the responsibilities which inevitably follow permanent limitation of the independence of other peoples. Superficial observers seem to find no destiny for our abounding increase in population, in wealth and power except that of imperialism. They fail to see that the American people are engrossed in the building for themselves of a new economic system, a new social system, a new political system — all of which are characterized by aspirations of freedom of opportunity and thereby are the negation of imperialism. They fail to realize that because of our abounding prosperity our youth are pressing more and more into our institutions of learning; that our people are seeking a larger vision through art, literature, science, and travel; that they are moving toward stronger moral and spiritual life — that from these things our sympathies are broadening beyond the bounds of our Nation and race toward their true expression in a real brotherhood of man. They fail to see that the idealism of America will lead it to no narrow or selfish channel, but inspire it to do its full share as a nation toward the advancement of civilization. It will do that not by mere declaration but by taking a practical part in supporting all useful international undertakings. We not only desire peace with the world, but to see peace maintained throughout the world. We wish to advance the reign of justice and reason toward the extinction of force.

The recent treaty for the renunciation of war as an instrument of national policy sets an advanced standard in our conception of the relations of nations. Its acceptance should pave the way to greater limitation of armament, the offer of which we sincerely extend to the world. But its full realization also implies a greater and greater perfection in the instrumentalities for pacific settlement of controversies between nations. In the creation and use of these instrumentalities we should support every sound method of conciliation, arbitration, and judicial settlement. American statesmen were among the first to propose and they have constantly urged upon the world, the establishment of a tribunal for the settlement of controversies of a justiciable character. The Permanent Court of International Justice in its major purpose is thus peculiarly identified with American ideals and with American statesmanship. No more potent instrumentality for this purpose has ever been conceived and no other is practicable of establishment. The reservations placed upon our adherence should not be misinterpreted. The United States seeks by these reservations no special privilege or advantage but only to clarify our relation to advisory opinions and other matters which are subsidiary to the major purpose of the court. The way should, and I believe will, be found by which we may take our proper place in a movement so fundamental to the progress of peace.

Our people have determined that we should make no political engagements such as membership in the League of Nations, which may commit us in advance as a nation to become involved in the settlements of controversies between other countries. They adhere to the belief that the independence of America from such obligations increases its ability and availability for service in all fields of human progress.

I have lately returned from a journey among our sister Republics of the Western Hemisphere. I have received unbounded hospitality and courtesy as their expression of friendliness to our country. We are held by particular bonds of sympathy and common interest with them. They are each of them building a racial character and a culture which is an impressive contribution to human progress. We wish only for the maintenance of their independence, the growth of their stability, and their prosperity. While we have had wars in the Western Hemisphere, yet on the whole the record is in encouraging contrast with that of other parts of the world. Fortunately the New World is largely free from the inheritances of fear and distrust which have so troubled the Old World. We should keep it so.

It is impossible, my countrymen, to speak of peace without profound emotion. In thousands of homes in America, in millions of homes around the world, there are vacant chairs. It would be a shameful confession of our unworthiness if it should develop that we have abandoned the hope for which all these men died. Surely civilization is old enough, surely mankind is mature enough so that we ought in our own lifetime to find a way to permanent peace. Abroad, to west and east, are nations whose sons mingled their blood with the blood of our sons on the battle fields. Most of these nations have contributed to our race, to our culture, our knowledge, and our progress. From one of them we derive our very language and from many of them much of the genius of our institutions. Their desire for peace is as deep and sincere as our own.

Peace can be contributed to by respect for our ability in defense. Peace can be promoted by the limitation of arms and by the creation of the instrumentalities for peaceful settlement of controversies. But it will become a reality only through self-restraint and active effort in friendliness and helpfulness. I covet for this administration a record of having further contributed to advance the cause of peace.

PARTY RESPONSIBILITIES

In our form of democracy the expression of the popular will can be effected only through the instrumentality of political parties. We maintain party government not to promote intolerant partisanship but because opportunity must be given for expression of the popular will, and organization provided for the execution of its mandates and for accountability of government to the people. It follows that the Government both in the executive and the legislative branches must carry out in good faith the platforms upon which the party was intrusted with power. But the government is that of the whole people; the party is the instrument through which policies are determined and men chosen to bring them into being. The animosities of elections should have no place in our Government, for government must concern itself alone with the common weal.

SPECIAL SESSION OF THE CONGRESS

Action upon some of the proposals upon which the Republican Party was returned to power, particularly further agricultural relief and limited changes in the tariff, can not in justice to our farmers, our labor, and our manufacturers be postponed. I shall therefore request a special session of Congress for the consideration of these two questions. I shall deal with each of them upon the assembly of the Congress.

OTHER MANDATES FROM THE ELECTION

It appears to me that the more important further mandates from the recent election were the maintenance of the integrity of the Constitution; the vigorous enforcement of the laws; the continuance of economy in public expenditure; the continued regulation of business to prevent domination in the community; the denial of ownership or operation of business by the Government in competition with its citizens; the avoidance of policies which would involve us in the controversies of foreign nations; the more effective reorganization of the departments of the Federal Government; the expansion of public works; and the promotion of welfare activities affecting education and the home.

These were the more tangible determinations of the election, but beyond them was the confidence and belief of the people that we would not neglect the support of the embedded ideals and aspirations of America. These ideals and aspirations are the touchstones upon which the day-to-day administration and legislative acts of government must be tested. More than this, the Government must, so far as lies within its proper powers, give leadership to the realization of these ideals and to the fruition of these aspirations. No one can adequately reduce these things of the spirit to phrases or to a catalogue of definitions. We do know what the attainments of these ideals should be: The preservation of self-government and its full foundations in local government; the perfection of justice whether in economic or in social fields; the maintenance of ordered liberty; the denial of domination by any group or class; the building up and preservation of equality of opportunity; the stimulation of initiative and individuality; absolute integrity in public affairs; the choice of officials for fitness to office; the direction of economic progress toward prosperity and the further lessening of poverty; the freedom of public opinion; the sustaining of education and of the advancement of knowledge; the growth of religious spirit and the tolerance of all faiths; the strengthening of the home; the advancement of peace.

There is no short road to the realization of these aspirations. Ours is a progressive people, but with a determination that progress must be based upon the foundation of experience. Ill-considered remedies for our faults bring only penalties after them. But if we hold the faith of the men in our mighty past who created these ideals, we shall leave them heightened and strengthened for our children.

CONCLUSION

This is not the time and place for extended discussion. The questions before our country are problems of progress to higher standards; they are not the problems of degeneration. They demand thought and they serve to quicken the conscience and enlist our sense of responsibility for their settlement. And that responsibility rests upon you, my countrymen, as much as upon those of us who have been selected for office.

Ours is a land rich in resources; stimulating in its glorious beauty; filled with millions of happy homes; blessed with comfort and opportunity. In no nation are the institutions of progress more advanced. In no nation are the fruits of accomplishment more secure. In no nation is the government more worthy of respect. No country is more loved by its people. I have an abiding faith in their capacity, integrity and high purpose. I have no fears for the future of our country. It is bright with hope.

In the presence of my countrymen, mindful of the solemnity of this occasion, knowing what the task means and the responsibility which it involves, I beg your tolerance, your aid, and your cooperation. I ask the help of Almighty God in this service to my country to which you have called me.

FIRST ANNUAL MESSAGE TO CONGRESS
December 3, 1929

In this message Hoover declares his belief that business confidence has already been reestablished in the nation since the collapse on October 24, 1929, of the New York stock market and the onset of the subsequent economic crisis.

To the Senate and House of Representatives:

The Constitution requires that the President "shall, from time to time, give to the Congress information of the state of the Union, and recommend to their consideration such measures as he shall judge necessary and expedient." In complying with that requirement I wish to emphasize that during the past year the Nation has continued to grow in strength; our people have advanced in comfort; we have gained in knowledge; the education of youth has been more widely spread; moral and spiritual forces have been maintained; peace has become more assured. The problems with which we are confronted are the problems of growth and of progress. In their solution we have to determine the facts, to develop the relative importance to be assigned to such facts, to formulate a common judgment upon them, and to realize solutions in a spirit of conciliation.

FOREIGN RELATIONS

We are not only at peace with all the world, but the foundations for future peace are being substantially strengthened. To promote peace is our long-established policy. Through the Kellogg-Briand pact a great moral standard has been raised in the world. By it fifty-four nations have covenanted to renounce war and to settle all disputes by pacific means. Through it a new world outlook has been inaugurated which has profoundly affected the foreign policies of nations. Since its inauguration we have initiated new efforts not only in the organization of the machinery of peace but also to eliminate dangerous forces which produce controversies amongst nations. . . .

GENERAL ECONOMIC SITUATION

The country has enjoyed a large degree of prosperity and sound progress during the past year with a steady improvement in methods of production and distribution and consequent advancement in standards of living. Progress has, of course, been unequal among industries, and some, such as coal, lumber, leather, and textiles, still lag behind. The long upward trend of fundamental progress, however, gave rise to over-optimism as to profits, which translated itself into a wave of uncontrolled speculation in securities, resulting in the diversion of capital from business to the stock market and the inevitable crash. The natural consequences have been a reduction in the consumption of luxuries and semi-necessities by those who have met with losses, and a number of persons thrown temporarily out of employment. Prices of agricultural products dealt in upon the great markets have been affected in sympathy with the stock crash.

Fortunately, the Federal reserve system had taken measures to strengthen the position against the day when speculation would break, which together with the strong position of the banks has carried the whole credit system through the crisis without impairment. The capital which has been hitherto absorbed in stock-market loans for speculative purposes is now returning to the normal channels of business. There has been no inflation in the prices of commodities; there has been no undue accumulation of goods, and foreign trade has expanded to a magnitude which exerts a steadying influence upon activity in industry and employment.

The sudden threat of unemployment and especially the recollection of the economic consequences of previous crashes under a much less secured financial system created unwarranted pessimism and fear. It was recalled that past storms of similar character had resulted in retrenchment of construction, reduction of wages, and laying off of workers. The natural result was the tendency of business agencies throughout the country to pause in their plans and proposals for continuation and extension of their business, and this hesitation unchecked could in itself intensify into a depression with widespread unemployment and suffering.

I have, therefore, instituted systematic, voluntary measures of cooperation with the business institutions and with state and municipal authorities to make certain that fundamental businesses of the country shall continue as usual, that wages and therefore consuming power shall not be reduced, and that a special effort shall be made to expand construction work in order to assist in equalizing other deficits in employment. Due to the enlarged sense of cooperation and responsibility which has grown in the business world during the past few years the response has been remarkable and satisfactory. We have canvassed the Federal Government and instituted measures of prudent expansion in such work that should be helpful, and upon which the different departments will make some early recommendations to Congress.

I am convinced that through these measures we have reestablished confidence. Wages should remain stable. A very large degree of industrial unemployment and suffering which would otherwise have occurred has been prevented. Agricultural prices have reflected the returning confidence. The measures taken must be vigorously pursued until normal conditions are restored.

AGRICULTURE

The agricultural situation is improving. The gross farm income as estimated by the Department of Agriculture for the crop season 1926-27 was $12,100,000,000; for 1927-28 it was $12,300,000,000; for 1928-29 it was $12,500,000,000; and estimated on the basis of prices since the last harvest the value of the 1929-30 crop would be over $12,600,000,000. The slight decline in general commodity prices during the past few years naturally assists the farmers' buying power.

The number of farmer bankruptcies is very materially decreased below previous years. The decline in land values now seems to be arrested and rate of movement from the farm to the city has been reduced. Not all sections of agriculture, of course, have fared equally, and some areas have suffered from drought. Responsible farm leaders have assured me that a large measure of confidence is returning to agriculture and that a feeling of optimism pervades that industry.

The most extensive action for strengthening the agricultural industry ever taken by any government was inaugurated through the farm marketing act of June 15 last. Under its provisions the Federal Farm Board has been established, comprised of men long and widely experienced in agriculture and sponsored by the farm organizations of the country. During its short period of existence the board has taken definite steps toward a more efficient organization of agriculture, toward the elimination of waste in marketing, and toward the upbuilding of farmers' marketing organizations on sounder and more efficient lines. Substantial headway has been made in the organization of four of the basic commodities — grain, cotton, livestock, and wool. Support by the board to cooperative marketing organizations and other board activities undoubtedly have served to steady the farmers' market during the recent crisis and have operated also as a great stimulus to the cooperative organization of agriculture. The problems of the industry are most complex, and the need for sound organization is imperative. Yet the board is moving rapidly along the lines laid out for it in the act, facilitating the creation by farmers of farmer-owned and farmer-controlled organizations and federating them into central institutions, with a view to increasing the bargaining power of agriculture, preventing and controlling surpluses, and mobilizing the economic power of agriculture.

HERBERT HOOVER

The White House,
December 3, 1929

STATEMENT ON THE HAWLEY-SMOOT TARIFF BILL
June 15, 1930

*Hoover gives his reasons for intending to sign the Haw-
ley-Smoot Tariff Bill, which provided for the highest
tariff rates in the history of the nation. On May 4, 1930,
Hoover received a petition signed by 1,028 prominent
economists, opposing the passage of the protective tariff
bill and urging a Presidential veto if the Congress approved the measure. The petition argued that the high
rates would sharply reduce American trade, a situation
particularly harmful during the Depression. He signed the
Hawley-Smoot Tariff Bill on June 17, 1930. Within 3 years
33 foreign countries retaliated against the high rates by
increasing their rates on American products.*

Statement by the President:

I shall approve the Tariff Bill. This legislation has now been under
almost continuous consideration by Congress for nearly fifteen months.
It was undertaken as the result of pledges given by the Republican
Party at Kansas City. Its declarations embraced these obligations:

"The Republican Party believes that the home market
built up under the protective policy belongs to the American farmer, and it pledges its support of legislation which
will give this market to him to the full extent of his ability
to supply it.

"There are certain industries which cannot now successfully compete with foreign producers because of lower
foreign wages and a lower cost of living abroad, and we
pledge the next Republican Congress to an examination and
where necessary a revision of these schedules to the end
the American labor in these industries may again command
the home market, may maintain its standard of living, and
may count upon steady employment in its accustomed field."

Platform promises must not be empty gestures. In my message of
April 16, 1929, to the Special Session of the Congress I accordingly
recommended an increase in agricultural protection; a limited revision
of other schedules to take care of the economic changes necessitating
increases or decreases since the enactment of the 1922 law, and I
further recommended a reorganization of the Tariff Commission and of
the method of executing the flexible provisions.

A statistical estimate of the bill by the Tariff Commission shows
that the average duties collected under the 1922 Law were about 13.8%

of the value of all imports, both free and dutiable, while if the new law
had been applied it would have increased this percentage to about 16%.

This compares with the average level of the tariff under

The McKinley law of	23.0%
The Wilson law of	20.9%
The Dingley law of	25.8%
The Payne-Aldrich law of	19.3%
The Fordney-McCumber law of	13.83%

Under the Underwood law of 1913 the amounts were disturbed by
war conditions varying 6% to 14.8%.

The proportion of imports which will be free of duty under the
new law is estimated at from 61% to 63%. This compares with averages
under

The McKinley law of	52.4%
The Wilson law of	49.4%
The Dingley law of	45.2%
The Payne-Aldrich law of	52.5%
The Fordney-McCumber law of	63.8%

Under the Underwood law of 1913 disturbed conditions varied the
free list from 60% to 73% averaging 66.3%

The increases in tariff are largely directed to the interest of
the farmer. Of the increases, it is stated by the Tariff Commission that
93.73% are upon products of agricultural origin measured in value, as
distinguished from 6.25% upon commodities of strictly non-agricultural
origin. The average rate upon agricultural raw materials shows an increase from 38.10% to 48.92% in contrast to dutiable articles of strictly
other than agricultural origin which show an average increase of from
31.02% to 34.31%. Compensatory duties have necessarily been given on
products manufactured from agricultural raw materials and protective
rates added to these in some instances.

The extent of rate revision as indicated by the Tariff Commission
is that in value of the total imports the duties upon approximately 22.5%
have been increased, and 77.5% were untouched or decreased. By
number of the dutiable items mentioned in the bill out of the total of
about 3300 there were about 890 increased, 235 decreased, and 2170
untouched. The number of items increased was, therefore, 27% of all
dutiable items, and compares with 83% of the number of items which
were increased in the 1922 revision.

The Tariff Law is like all other tariff legislation, whether framed
primarily upon a protective or a revenue basis. It contains many compromises between sectional interests and between different industries.
No tariff bill has ever been enacted or ever will be enacted under the

present system, that will be perfect. A large portion of the items are always adjusted with good judgment, but it is bound to contain some inequalities and inequitable compromises. There are items upon which duties will prove too high and others upon which duties will prove to be too low.

Certainly no President, with his other duties, can pretend to make that exhaustive determination of the complex facts which surround each of those 3300 items, and which has required the attention of hundreds of men in Congress for nearly a year and a third. That responsibility must rest upon the Congress in a legislative rate revision.

On the administrative side I have insisted, however, that there should be created a new basis for the flexible tariff and it has been incorporated in this law. Thereby the means are established for objective and judicial review of these rates upon principles laid down by the Congress, free from pressures inherent in legislative action. Thus, the outstanding step of this tariff legislation has been the reorganization of the largely inoperative flexible provision of 1922 into a form which should render it possible to secure prompt and scientific adjustment of serious inequities and inequalities which may prove to have been incorporated in the bill.

This new provision has even a larger importance. If a perfect tariff bill were enacted today, the increased rapidity of economic change and the constant shifting of our relations to industries abroad, will create a continuous stream of items which would work hardship upon some segment of the American people except for the provision of this relief. Without a workable flexible provision we would require even more frequent congressional tariff revision than during the past. With it the country should be freed from further general revision for many years to come. Congressional revisions are not only disturbing to business but with all their necessary collateral surroundings in lobbies, log rolling and the activities of group interests, are disturbing to public confidence.

Under the old flexible provisions, the task of adjustment was imposed directly upon the President, and the limitations in the law which circumscribed it were such that action was long delayed and it was largely inoperative, although important benefits were brought to the dairying, flax, glass, and other industries through it.

The new flexible provision established the responsibility for revisions upon a reorganized Tariff Commission, composed of members equally of both parties as a definite rate-making body acting through semi-judicial methods of open hearings and investigation by which items can be taken up one by one upon direction or upon application of aggrieved parties. Recommendations are to be made to the President, he being given authority to promulgate or veto the conclusions of the Commission. Such revision can be accomplished without disturbance to business, as they concern but one item at a time, and the principles laid down assure a protective basis.

The principle of a protective tariff for the benefit of labor, industry, and the farmer is established in the bill by the requirement that the Commission shall adjust the rates so as to cover the differences in cost of production at home and abroad — and it is authorized to increase or decrease the duties by 50% to effect this end. The means and methods of ascertaining such differences by the Commission are provided in such fashion as should expedite prompt and effective action if grievances develop.

When the flexible principle was first written into law in 1922, by tradition and force of habit the old conception of legislative revision was so firmly fixed that the innovation was bound to be used with caution and in a restricted field, even had it not been largely inoperative for other reasons. Now, however, and particularly after the record of the last fifteen months, there is a growing and widespread realization that in this highly complicated and intricately organized and rapidly shifting modern economic world, the time has come when a more scientific and businesslike method of tariff revision must be devised. Toward this the new flexible provision takes a long step.

These provisions meet the repeated demands of statemen and industrial and agricultural leaders over the past 25 years. It complies in full degree with the proposals made 20 years ago by President Roosevelt. It now covers proposals which I urged in 1922.

If, however, by any chance the flexible provisions now made should prove insufficient for effective action, I shall ask for further authority for the Commission, for I believe that public opinion will give wholehearted support to the carrying out of such a program on a generous scale to the end that we may develop a protective system free from the vices which have characterized every tariff revision in the past.

The complaints from some foreign countries that these duties have been placed unduly high can be remedied, if justified, by proper application to the Tariff Commission.

It is urgent that the uncertainties in the business world which have been added to by the long-extended debate of the measure should be ended. They can be ended only by completion of this bill. Meritorious demands for further protection to agriculture and labor which have developed since the tariff of 1922 would not end if this bill fails of enactment. Agitation for legislative tariff revision would necessarily continue before the country. Nothing would contribute to retard business recovery more than this continued agitation.

As I have said, I do not assume the rate structure in this or any other tariff bill is perfect, but I am convinced that the disposal of the whole question is urgent. I believe that the flexible provisions can within reasonable time remedy inequalities; that this provision is a progressive advance and gives great hope of taking the tariff away from politics, lobbying, and log rolling; that the bill gives protection to agriculture for the market of its products and to several industries in need of such protection for the wage of their labor; that with returning normal conditions our foreign trade will continue to expand.

SECOND ANNUAL MESSAGE TO CONGRESS
December 2, 1930

*In this message Hoover, in addition to briefly treating a
number of topics of national concern, asks of Congress an
appropriation of from $100 million to $150 million for the
construction of public works to alleviate unemployment
during the Depression. On December 20, 1930, the Congress responded favorably to the request by authorizing
the expenditure of $116 million to execute the program*

To the Senate and House of Representatives:

I have the honor to comply with the requirement of the Constitution
that I should lay before the Congress information as to the state of the
Union, and recommend consideration of such measures as are necessary and expedient.

Substantial progress has been made during the year in national
peace and security; the fundamental strength of the Nation's economic
life is unimpaired; education and scientific discovery have made advances; our country is more alive to its problems of moral and spiritual welfare.

ECONOMIC SITUATION

During the past 12 months we have suffered with other nations
from economic depression.

The origins of this depression lie to some extent within our own
borders through a speculative period which diverted capital and energy
into speculation rather than constructive enterprise. Had overspecu-
lation in securities been the only force operating, we should have seen
recovery many months ago, as these particular dislocations have generally readjusted themselves.

Other deep-seated causes have been in action, however, chiefly
the world-wide overproduction beyond even the demand of prosperous
times for such important basic commodities as wheat, rubber, coffee,
sugar, copper, silver, zinc, to some extent cotton, and other raw
materials. The cumulative effects of demoralizing price falls of these
important commodities in the process of adjustment of production to
world consumption have produced financial crises in many countries
and have diminished the buying power of these countries for imported
goods to a degree which extended the difficulties farther afield by
creating unemployment in all the industrial nations. The political agitation in Asia; revolutions in South America and political unrest in
some European States; the methods of sale by Russia of her increasing

agricultural exports to European markets; and our own drought –
have all contributed to prolong and deepen the depression.

In the larger view the major forces of the depression now lie outside of the United States, and our recuperation has been retarded by
the unwarranted degree of fear and apprehension created by these
outside forces.

The extent of the depression is indicated by the following approxi-
mate percentages of activity during the past three months as compared
with the highly prosperous year of 1928:

> Value of department-store sales . . . . . 93% of 1928
> Volume of manufacturing production. . . 80% of 1928
> Volume of mineral production . . . . 90% of 1928
> Volume of factory employment . . . . . . 84% of 1928
> Total of bank deposits . . . . .105% of 1928
> Wholesale prices—all commodities . . . . 83% of 1928
> Cost of living . . . . 94% of 1928

Various other indexes indicate total decrease of activity from 1928
of from 15 to 20 per cent.

There are many factors which give encouragement for the future.
The fact that we are holding from 80 to 85 per cent of our normal activities and incomes; that our major financial and industrial institutions have come through the storm unimpaired; that price levels of
major commodities have remained approximately stable for some time;
that a number of industries are showing signs of increasing demand;
that the world at large is readjusting itself to the situation; all reflect
grounds for confidence. We should remember that these occasions
have been met many times before, that they are but temporary, that
our country is today stronger and richer in resources, in equipment,
in skill, than ever in its history. We are in an extraordinary degree
self-sustaining, we will overcome world influences and will lead the
march of prosperity as we have always done hitherto.

Economic depression can not be cured by legislative action or
executive pronouncement. Economic wounds must be healed by the
action of the cells of the economic body – the producers and consumers
themselves. Recovery can be expedited and its effects mitigated by
cooperative action. That cooperation requires that every individual
should sustain faith and courage; that each should maintain his self-
reliance; that each and every one should search for methods of improving his business or service; that the vast majority whose income
is unimpaired should not hoard out of fear but should pursue their
normal living and recreations; that each should seek to assist his
neighbors who may be less fortunate; that each industry should assist
its own employees; that each community and each state should assume
its full responsibilities for organization of employment and relief of

distress with that sturdiness and independence which built a great Nation.

Our people are responding to these impulses in remarkable degree.

The best contribution of government lies in encouragement of this voluntary cooperation in the community. The Government, National, state, and local, can join with the community in such programs and do its part. A year ago I, together with other officers of the Government, initiated extensive cooperative measures throughout the country.

The first of these measures was an agreement of leading employers to maintain the standards of wages and of labor leaders to use their influence against strife. In a large sense these undertakings have been adhered to and we have not witnessed the usual reductions of wages which have always heretofore marked depressions. The index of union wage scales shows them to be today fully up to the level of any of the previous three years. In consequence the buying power of the country has been much larger than would otherwise have been the case. Of equal importance the Nation has had unusual peace in industry and freedom from the public disorder which has characterized previous depressions.

The second direction of cooperation has been that our governments, National, state, and local, the industries and business so distribute employment as to give work to the maximum number of employees.

The third direction of cooperation has been to maintain and even extend construction work and betterments in anticipation of the future. It has been the universal experience in previous depressions that public works and private construction have fallen off rapidly with the general tide of depression. On this occasion, however, the increased authorization and generous appropriations by the Congress and the action of states and municipalities have resulted in the expansion of public construction to an amount even above that in the most prosperous years. In addition the cooperation of public utilities, railways, and other large organizations has been generously given in construction and betterment work in anticipation of future need. The Department of Commerce advises me that as a result, the volume of this type of construction work, which amounted to roughly $6,300,000,000 in 1929, instead of decreasing will show a total of about $7,000,000,000 for 1930. There has, of course, been a substantial decrease in the types of construction which could not be undertaken in advance of need.

The fourth direction of cooperation was the organization in such states and municipalities, as was deemed necessary, of committees to organize local employment, to provide for employment agencies, and to effect relief of distress.

The result of magnificent cooperation throughout the country has been that actual suffering has been kept to a minimum during the past 12 months, and our unemployment has been far less in proportion than in other large industrial countries. Some time ago it became evident that unemployment would continue over the winter and would necessarily be added to from seasonal causes and that the savings of workpeople would be more largely depleted. We have as a nation a definite duty to see that no deserving person in our country suffers from hunger or cold. I therefore set up a more extensive organization to stimulate more intensive cooperation throughout the country. There has been a most gratifying degree of response, from governors, mayors, and other public officials, from welfare organizations, and from employers in concerns both large and small. The local communities through their voluntary agencies have assumed the duty of relieving individual distress and are being generously supported by the public.

The number of those wholly out of employment seeking for work was accurately determined by the census last April as about 2,500,000. The Department of Labor index of employment in the larger trades shows some decrease in employment since that time. The problem from a relief point of view is somewhat less than the published estimates of the number of unemployed would indicate. The intensive community and individual efforts in providing special employment outside the listed industries are not reflected in the statistical indexes and tend to reduce such published figures. Moreover, there is estimated to be a constant figure at all times of nearly 1,000,000 unemployed who are not without annual income but temporarily idle in the shift from one job to another. We have an average of about three breadwinners to each two families, so that every person unemployed does not represent a family without income. The view that the relief problems are less than the gross numbers would indicate is confirmed by the experience of several cities, which shows that the number of families in distress represents from 10 to 20 per cent of the number of the calculated unemployed. This is not said to minimize the very real problem which exists but to weigh its actual proportions.

As a contribution to the situation the Federal Government is engaged upon the greatest program of waterway, harbor, flood control, public building, highway, and airway improvement in all our history. This, together with loans to merchant shipbuilders, improvement of the Navy and in military aviation, and other construction work of the Government will exceed $520,000,000 for this fiscal year. This compares with $253,000,000 in the fiscal year 1928. The construction works already authorized and the continuation of policies in Government aid will require a continual expenditure upwards of half a billion dollars annually.

I favor still further temporary expansion of these activities in aid to unemployment during this winter. The Congress will, however, have presented to it numbers of projects, some of them under the guise of, rather than the reality of, their usefulness in the increase of employment during the depression. There are certain common-sense limitations upon any expansions of construction work. The Government must not undertake works that are not of sound economic purpose and that have not been subject to searching technical investigation, and which have not been given adequate consideration by the Congress. The volume of construction work in the Government is already at the maximum limit warranted by financial prudence as a continuing policy. To increase taxation for purposes of construction work defeats its own purpose, as such taxes directly diminish employment in private industry. Again any kind of construction requires, after its authorization, a considerable time before labor can be employed in which to make engineering, architectural, and legal preparations. Our immediate problem is the increase of employment for the next six months, and new plans which do not produce such immediate result or which extend commitments beyond this period are not warranted.

The enlarged rivers and harbors, public building, and highway plans authorized by the Congress last session, however, offer an opportunity for assistance by the temporary acceleration of construction of these programs even faster than originally planned, especially if the technical requirements of the laws which entail great delays could be amended in such fashion as to speed up acquirements of land and the letting of contracts.

With view, however, to the possible need for acceleration, we, immediately upon receiving those authorities from the Congress five months ago, began the necessary technical work in preparation for such possible eventuality. I have canvassed the departments of the Government as to the maximum amount that can be properly added to our present expenditure to accelerate all construction during the next six months, and I feel warranted in asking the Congress for an appropriation of from $100,000,000 to $150,000,000 to provide such further employment in this emergency. In connection therewith we need some authority to make enlarged temporary advances of Federal-highway aid to the states.

I recommend that this appropriation be made distributable to the different departments upon recommendation of a committee of the Cabinet and approval by the President. Its application to works already authorized by the Congress assures its use in directions of economic importance and to public welfare. Such action will imply an expenditure upon construction of all kinds of over $650,000,000 during the next twelve months.

AGRICULTURE

The world-wide depression has affected agriculture in common with all other industries. The average price of farm produce has fallen to about 80 per cent of the levels of 1928. This average is, however, greatly affected by wheat and cotton, which have participated in world-wide overproduction and have fallen to about 60 per cent of the average price of the year 1928. Excluding these commodities, the prices of all other agricultural products are about 84 per cent of those of 1928. The average wholesale prices of other primary goods, such as nonferrous metals, have fallen to 76 per cent of 1928.

The price levels of our major agricultural commodities are, in fact, higher than those in other principal producing countries, due to the combined result of the tariff and the operations of the Farm Board. For instance, wheat prices at Minneapolis are about 30 per cent higher than at Winnipeg, and at Chicago they are about 20 per cent higher than at Buenos Aires. Corn prices at Chicago are over twice as high as at Buenos Aires. Wool prices average more than 80 per cent higher in this country than abroad, and butter is 30 per cent higher in New York City than in Copenhagen.

Aside from the misfortune to agriculture of the world-wide depression we have had the most severe drought. It has affected particularly the states bordering on the Potomac, Ohio, and Lower Mississippi Rivers, with some areas in Montana, Kansas, Oklahoma, and Texas. It has found its major expression in the shortage of pasturage and a shrinkage in the corn crop from an average of about 2,800,000,000 bushels to about 2,090,000,000 bushels.

On August 14 I called a conference of the governors of the most acutely affected states, and as a result of its conclusions I appointed a national committee comprising the heads of the important Federal agencies under the chairmanship of the Secretary of Agriculture. The governors in turn have appointed state committees representative of the farmers, bankers, business men, and the Red Cross, and subsidiary committees have been established in most of the acutely affected counties. Railway rates were reduced on feed and livestock in and out of the drought areas, and over 50,000 cars of such products have been transported under these reduced rates. The Red Cross established a preliminary fund of $5,000,000 for distress relief purposes and established agencies for its administration in each county. Of this fund less than $500,000 has been called for up to this time as the need will appear more largely during the winter. The Federal Farm Loan Board has extended its credit facilities, and the Federal Farm Board has given financial assistance to all affected cooperatives.

In order that the Government may meet its full obligation toward our countrymen in distress through no fault of their own, I recommend that an appropriation should be made to the Department of Agriculture to be loaned for the purpose of seed and feed for animals. Its application should as hitherto in such loans be limited to a gross amount to any one individual, and secured upon the crop.

The Red Cross can relieve the cases of individual distress by the sympathetic assistance of our people. . . .

HERBERT HOOVER

The White House,
December 2, 1930

MESSAGE TO CONGRESS ON THE REPORT OF THE WICKERSHAM COMMISSION
January 20, 1931

Hoover submits to Congress the report of the National Commission on Law Observance and Enforcement, familiarly known as the Wickersham Commission. On May 28, 1929, Hoover announced the appointment of that body, with former Attorney General George W. Wickersham as chairman, to conduct an investigation of prohibition and related problems of law enforcement. In its report the Commission declared that the enforcement of prohibition was hindered by widespread public antipathy and by the prospect of quick and large profits from participating in the manufacture and transportation of illegal alcoholic beverages. The Commission opposed the repeal of the 18th (Prohibition) Amendment to the Constitution, although a majority of its members favored its revision. In his message to Congress transmitting the report of the .Wickersham Commission Hoover states his opposition to the repeal of the 18th Amendment.

To the Congress:

The first deficiency appropriation act of March 4, 1929, carried an appropriation for a thorough investigation into the enforcement of the prohibition laws, together with the enforcement of other laws.

In pursuance of this provision I appointed a commission consisting of former Attorney General George W. Wickersham, chairman, former Secretary of War Newton D. Baker, Federal Judges William S. Kenyon, Paul J. McCormick, and William I. Grubb, former Chief Justice Kenneth Mackintosh of Supreme Court of Washington, Dean Roscoe Pound of Harvard Law School, President Ada L. Comstock of Radcliffe College, Henry W. Anderson of Virginia, Monte M. Lemann of New Orleans, and Frank J. Loesch of Chicago.

The commission thus comprises an able group of distinguished citizens of character and independence of thought, representative of different sections of the country. For 18 months they have exhaustively and painstakingly gathered and examined the facts as to enforcement, the benefits, and the abuses under the prohibition laws, both before and since the passage of the eighteenth amendment. I am transmitting their report immediately. Reports upon the enforcement of other criminal laws will follow.

The commission considers that the conditions of enforcement of the prohibition laws in the country as a whole are unsatisfactory but it reports that the Federal participation in enforcement has shown continued improvement since and as a consequence of the act of Congress of 1927 placing prohibition officers under civil service, and the act of 1930 transferring prohibition enforcement from the Treasury to the Department of Justice, and it outlines further possible improvement. It calls attention to the urgency of obedience to law by our citizens and to the imperative necessity for greater assumption and performance by state and local governments of their share of responsibilities under the "concurrent enforcement" provision of the Constitution if enforcement is to be successful. It recommends that further and more effective efforts be made to enforce the laws. It makes recommendations as to Federal administrative methods and certain secondary legislation for further increase of personnel, new classification of offenses, relief of the courts, and amendments to the national prohibition,act clarifying the law and eliminating irritations which arise under it. Some of these recommendations have been enacted by the Congress or are already in course of legislation. I commend these suggestions to the Congress at an appropriate time.

The commission, by a large majority, does not favor the repeal of the eighteenth amendment as a method of cure for the inherent abuses of the liquor traffic. I am in accord with this view. I am in unity with the spirit of the report in seeking constructive steps to advance the national ideal of eradication of the social and economic and political evils of this traffic, to preserve the gains which have been made, and to eliminate the abuses which exist, at the same time facing with an open mind the difficulties which have arisen under this experiment. I do, however, see serious objection to, and therefore must not be understood as recommending, the commission's proposed revision of the eighteenth amendment which is suggested by them for possible consideration at some future time if the continued effort at enforcement should not prove successful. My own duty and that of all executive officials is clear — to enforce the law with all the means at our disposal without equivocation or reservation.

The report is the result of a thorough and comprehensive study of the situation by a representative and authoritative group. It clearly recognizes the gains which have been made and is resolute that those gains shall be preserved. There are necessarily differences in views among its members. It is a temperate and judicial presentation. It should stimulate the clarification of public mind and the advancement of public thought.

HERBERT HOOVER

The White House
January 20, 1931

VETO OF THE MUSCLE SHOALS BILL
March 3, 1931

Hoover vetoes the bill of Republican Senator George Norris of Nebraska, providing for a federal public works project at Muscle Shoals on the Tennessee River, on the ground of his opposition "to the Government entering any business . . . in competition with our citizens." The Congress sustained the Presidential veto. On May 25, 1928, President Calvin Coolidge vetoed a similar bill sponsored by Norris on the same ground that such a government operation would compete with private enterprise. Norris ultimately achieved success when President Franklin D. Roosevelt signed on May 18, 1933, the Tennessee Valley Authority Bill creating the Tennessee Valley Authority (TVA) and providing for the construction of dams and power plants to develop the Tennessee River Valley.

To the Senate:

I return herewith, without my approval, Senate Joint Resolution 49, "To provide for the national defense by the creation of a corporation for the operation of the Government properties at and near Muscle Shoals in the State of Alabama; to authorize the letting of the Muscle Shoals properties under certain conditions; and for other purposes."

This bill proposes the transformation of the war plant at Muscle Shoals, together with important expansions, into a permanently operated Government institution for the production and distribution of power and the manufacture of fertilizers. . . .

I am firmly opposed to the Government entering into any business the major purpose of which is competition with our citizens. There are national emergencies which require that the Government should temporarily enter the field of business, but they must be emergency actions and in matters where the cost of the project is secondary to much higher considerations. There are many localities where the Federal Government is justified in the construction of great dams and reservoirs, where navigation, flood control, reclamation or stream regulation are of dominant importance, and where they are beyond the capacity or purpose of private or local government capital to construct. In these cases power is often a by-product and should be disposed of by contract or lease. But for the Federal Government deliberately to go out to build up and expand such an occasion to the major purpose of a power and manufacturing business is to break down the initiative and enterprise of the American people; it is destruction of equality of opportunity amongst our people; it is the negation of the ideals upon which our civilization has been based.

This bill raises one of the important issues confronting our people. That is squarely the issue of Federal Government ownership and operation of power and manufacturing business not as a minor by-product but as a major purpose. Involved in this question is the agitation against the conduct of the power industry. The power problem is not to be solved by the Federal Government going into the power business, nor is it to be solved by the project in this bill. The remedy for abuses in the conduct of that industry lies in regulation and not by the Federal Government entering upon the business itself. I have recommended to the Congress on various occasions that action should be taken to establish Federal regulation of interstate power in cooperation with state authorities. This bill would launch the Federal Government upon a policy ownership and operation of power utilities upon a basis of competition instead of by the proper Government function of regulation for the protection of all the people. I hesitate to contemplate the future of our institutions, of our government, and of our country if the preoccupation of its officials is to be no longer the promotion of justice and equal opportunity but is to be devoted to barter in the markets. That is not liberalism, it is degeneration.

This proposal can be effectively opposed upon other and perhaps narrower grounds. The establishment of a Federal-operated power business and fertilizer factory in the Tennessee Valley means Federal control from Washington with all the vicissitudes of national politics and the tyrannies of remote bureaucracy imposed upon the people of that valley without voice by them in their own resources, the overriding of state and local government, the undermining of state and local responsibility. The very history of this project over the past 10 years should be a complete demonstration of the ineptness of the Federal Government to administer such enterprise and of the penalties which the local community suffers under it.

This bill distinctly proposes to enter the field of powers reserved to the states. It would deprive the adjacent states of the right to control rates for this power and would deprive them of taxes on property within their borders and would invade and weaken the authority of local government.

Aside from the wider issues involved the immediate effect of this legislation would be that no other development of power could take place on the Tennessee River with the Government in that field. That river contains two or three millions of potential horsepower, but the threat of the subjection of that area to a competition which under this bill carries no responsibility to earn interest on the investment or taxes would either destroy the possibility of private development of the great resources of the river or alternately impose the extension of this development upon the Federal Government. It would appear that this latter is the course desired by many proponents of this bill. There are many other objections which can be raised to this bill, of lesser importance but in themselves a warranty for its disapproval.

It must be understood that these criticisms are directed to the project as set up in this bill; they are not directed to the possibilities of a project denuded of uneconomic and unsound provisions nor is it a reflection upon the value of these resources.

I sympathize greatly with the desire of the people of Tennessee and Alabama to see this great asset turned to practical use. It can be so turned and to their benefit. I am loath to leave a subject of this character without a suggestion for solution. Congress has been thwarted for 10 years in finding solution, by rivalry of private interests and by the determination of certain groups to commit the Federal Government to Government ownership and operation of power.

The real development of the resources and the industries of the Tennessee Valley can only be accomplished by the people in that valley themselves. Muscle Shoals can only be administered by the people upon the ground, responsible to their own communities, directing them solely for the benefit of their communities and not for purposes of pursuit of social theories or national politics. Any other course deprives them of liberty.

I would therefore suggest that the States of Alabama and Tennessee who are the ones primarily concerned should set up a commission of their own representatives together with a representative from the national farm organizations and the Corps of Army Engineers; that there be vested in that commission full authority to lease the plants at Muscle Shoals in the interest of the local community and agriculture generally. It could lease the nitrate plants to the advantage of agriculture. The power plant is today earning a margin over operating expenses. Such a commission could increase this margin without further capital outlay and should be required to use all such margins for the benefit of agriculture.

The Federal Government should, as in the case of Boulder Canyon, construct Cove Creek Dam as a regulatory measure for the flood protection of the Tennessee Valley and the development of its water resources, but on the same bases as those imposed at Boulder Canyon — that is, that construction should be undertaken at such time as the proposed commission is able to secure contracts for use of the increased water supply to power users or the lease of the power produced as a by-product from such a dam on terms that will return to the Government interest upon its outlay with amortization. On this basis the Federal Government will have cooperated to place the question into the hands of the people primarily concerned. They can lease as their wisdom dictates and for the industries that they deem best

in their own interest. It would get a war relic out of politics and into
the realm of service.

						HERBERT HOOVER

The White House,
March 3, 1931

THIRD ANNUAL MESSAGE TO CONGRESS
December 8, 1931

In this message Hoover recommends to Congress, among other things, that it pass 2 pieces of legislation, 1 establishing an emergency reconstruction finance corporation and the other providing for a system of federal home loan banks. Both of his recommendations became accomplished facts. On January 22, 1932, Hoover signed the bill establishing the Reconstruction Finance Corporation to provide federal government loans to banks, railroads, and insurance companies. On July 22, 1932, he signed the Federal Home Loan Bank Bill establishing a number of home loan banks throughout the nation to make loans to mortgage-lending institutions in order to stimulate residential construction and thus increase employment.

To the Senate and House of Representatives:

It is my duty under the Constitution to transmit to the Congress information on the state of the Union and to recommend for its consideration necessary and expedient measures.

The chief influence affecting the state of the Union during the past year has been the continued world-wide economic disturbance. Our national concern has been to meet the emergencies it has created for us and to lay the foundations for recovery.

If we lift our vision beyond these immediate emergencies we find fundamental national gains even amid depression. In meeting the problems of this difficult period, we have witnessed a remarkable development of the sense of cooperation in the community. For the first time in the history of our major economic depressions there has been a notable absence of public disorders and industrial conflict. Above all there is an enlargement of social and spiritual responsibility among the people. The strains and stresses upon business have resulted in closer application, in saner policies, and in better methods. Public improvements have been carried out on a larger scale than even in normal times. The country is richer in physical property, in newly discovered resources, and in productive capacity than ever before. There has been constant gain in knowledge and education; there has been continuous advance in science and invention; there has been distinct gain in public health. Business depressions have been recurrent in the life of our country and are but transitory. The Nation has emerged from each of them with increased strength and virility because of the enlightenment they have brought, the readjustments and the larger understanding of the realities and obligations of life and work which come from them.

FOREIGN AFFAIRS

We are at peace with the world. We have cooperated with other nations to preserve peace. The rights of our citizens abroad have been protected.

The economic depression has continued and deepened in every part of the world during the past year. In many countries political instability, excessive armaments, debts, governmental expenditures, and taxes have resulted in revolutions, in unbalanced budgets and monetary collapse and financial panics, in dumping of goods upon world markets, and in diminished consumption of commodities.

Within two years there have been revolutions or acute social disorders in 19 countries, embracing more than half the population of the world. Ten countries have been unable to meet their external obligations. In 14 countries, embracing a quarter of the world's population, former monetary standards have been temporarily abandoned. In a number of countries there have been acute financial panics or compulsory restraints upon banking. These disturbances have many roots in the dislocations from the World War. Every one of them has reacted upon us. They have sharply affected the markets and prices of our agricultural and industrial products. They have increased unemployment and greatly embarrassed our financial and credit system.

As our difficulties during the past year have plainly originated in large degree from these sources, any effort to bring about our own recuperation has dictated the necessity of cooperation by us with other nations in reasonable effort to restore world confidence and economic stability.

Cooperation of our Federal reserve system and our banks with the central banks in foreign countries has contributed to localize and ameliorate a number of serious financial crises or moderate the pressures upon us and thus avert disasters which would have affected us.

The economic crisis in Germany and Central Europe last June rose to the dimensions of a general panic from which it was apparent that without assistance these nations must collapse. Apprehensions of such collapse had demoralized our agricultural and security markets and so threatened other nations as to impose further dangers upon us. But of highest importance was the necessity of cooperation on our part to relieve the people of Germany from imminent disasters and to maintain their important relations to progress and stability in the world. Upon the initiative of this Government a year's postponement of reparations and other inter-governmental debts was brought about. Upon our further initiative an agreement was made by Germany's private creditors providing for an extension of such credits until the German people can develop more permanent and definite forms of relief.

We have continued our policy of withdrawing our marines from Haiti and Nicaragua.

The difficulties between China and Japan have given us great concern, not alone for the maintenance of the spirit of the Kellogg-Briand Pact, but for the maintenance of the treaties to which we are a party assuring the territorial integrity of China. It is our purpose to assist in finding solutions sustaining the full spirit of those treaties.

I shall deal at greater length with our foreign relations in a later message.

THE DOMESTIC SITUATION

Many undertakings have been organized and forwarded during the past year to meet the new and changing emergencies which have constantly confronted us.

Broadly the community has cooperated to meet the needs of honest distress, and to take such emergency measures as would sustain confidence in our financial system and would cushion the violence of liquidation in industry and commerce, thus giving time for orderly readjustment of costs, inventories, and credits without panic and widespread bankruptcy. These measures have served those purposes and will promote recovery.

In these measures we have striven to mobilize and stimulate private initiative and local and community responsibility. There has been the least possible Government entry into the economic field, and that only in temporary and emergency form. Our citizens and our local governments have given a magnificent display of unity and action, initiative and patriotism in solving a multitude of difficulties and in cooperating with the Federal Government.

For a proper understanding of my recommendations to the Congress it is desirable very briefly to review such activities during the past year.

The emergencies of unemployment have been met by action in many directions. The appropriations for the continued speeding up of the great Federal construction program have provided direct and indirect aid to employment upon a large scale. By organized unity of action, the states and municipalities have also maintained large programs of public improvement. Many industries have been prevailed upon to anticipate and intensify construction. Industrial concerns and other employers have been organized to spread available work amongst all their employees, instead of discharging a portion of them. A large majority have maintained wages at as high levels as the safe conduct of their business would permit. This course has saved us from industrial conflict and disorder which have characterized all previous depressions. Immigration has been curtailed by administrative action. Upon the basis of normal immigration the decrease amounts to about 300,000 individuals who otherwise would have been added to our employment. The expansion of Federal employment agencies under appropriations by the Congress has proved most effective. Through the President's organization for unemployment relief, public and private agencies were successfully mobilized last winter to provide employment and other measures against distress. Similar organization gives assurance against suffering during the coming winter. Committees of leading citizens are now active at practically every point of unemployment. In the large majority they have been assured the funds necessary which, together with local government aids, will meet the situation. A few exceptional localities will be further organized. The evidence of the Public Health Service shows an actual decrease of sickness and infant and general mortality below normal years. No greater proof could be adduced that our people have been protected from hunger and cold and that the sense of social responsibility in the Nation has responded to the need of the unfortunate.

To meet the emergencies in agriculture the loans authorized by Congress for rehabilitation in the drought areas have enabled farmers to produce abundant crops in those districts. The Red Cross undertook and magnificently administered relief for over 2,500,000 drought sufferers last winter. It has undertaken this year to administer relief to 100,000 sufferers in the new drought area of certain northwest states. The action of the Federal Farm Board in granting credits to farm cooperatives saved many of them from bankruptcy and increased their purpose and strength. By enabling farm cooperatives to cushion the fall in prices of farm products in 1930 and 1931 the Board secured higher prices to the farmer than would have been obtained otherwise, although the benefits of this action were partially defeated by continued world overproduction. Incident to this action the failure of a large number of farmers and of country banks was averted which could quite possibly have spread into a major disaster. The banks in the South have cooperated with the Farm Board in creation of a pool for the better marketing of accumulated cotton. Growers have been materially assisted by this action. Constant effort has been made to reduce overproduction in relief of agriculture and to promote the foreign buying of agricultural products by sustaining economic stability abroad.

To meet our domestic emergencies in credit and banking arising from the reaction to acute crises abroad the National Credit Association was set up by the banks with resources of $500,000,000 to support sound banks against the frightened withdrawals and hoarding. It is giving aid to reopen solvent banks which have been closed. Federal officials have brought about many beneficial unions of banks and have employed other means which have prevented many bank closings. As a result of these measures the hoarding withdrawals which had risen to over $250,000,000 per week after the British crisis have substantially ceased.

FURTHER MEASURES

The major economic forces and weaknesses at home and abroad have now been exposed and can be appraised, and the time is ripe for forward action to expedite our recovery.

Although some of the causes of our depression are due to speculation, inflation of securities and real estate, unsound foreign investments, and mismanagement of financial institutions, yet our self-contained national economy, with its matchless strength and resources, would have enabled us to recover long since but for the continued dislocations, shocks, and setbacks from abroad.

Whatever the causes may be, the vast liquidation and readjustments which have taken place have left us with a large degree of credit paralysis, which together with the situation in our railways and the conditions abroad, are now the outstanding obstacles to recuperation. If we can put our financial resources to work and can ameliorate the financial situation in the railways, I am confident we can make a large measure of recovery independent of the rest of the world. A strong America is the highest contribution to world stability.

One phase of the credit situation is indicated in the banks. During the past year banks, representing 3 per cent of our total deposits have been closed. A large part of these failures have been caused by withdrawals for hoarding, as distinguished from the failures early in the depression where weakness due to mismanagement was the larger cause of failure. Despite their closing, many of them will pay in full. Although such withdrawals have practically ceased, yet $1,100,000,000 of currency was previously withdrawn which has still to return to circulation. This represents a large reduction of the ability of our banks to extend credit which would otherwise fertilize industry and agriculture. Furthermore, many of our bankers, in order to prepare themselves to meet possible withdrawals, have felt compelled to call in loans, to refuse new credits, and to realize upon securities, which in turn has demoralized the markets. The paralysis has been further augmented by the steady increase in recent years of the proportion of bank assets invested in long-term securities, such as mortgages and bonds. These securities tend to lose their liquidity in depression or temporarily to fall in value so that the ability of the banks to meet the shock of sudden withdrawal is greatly lessened and the restriction of all kinds of credit is thereby increased. The continuing credit paralysis has operated to accentuate the deflation and liquidation of commodities, real estate, and securities below any reasonable basis of values.

All of this tends to stifle business, especially the smaller units, and finally expresses itself in further depression of prices and values, in restriction on new enterprise, and in increased unemployment.

The situation largely arises from an unjustified lack of confidence. We have enormous volumes of idle money in the banks and in hoarding. We do not require more money or working capital — we need to put what we have to work.

The fundamental difficulties which have brought about financial strains in foreign countries do not exist in the United States. No external drain on our resources can threaten our position, because the balance of international payments is in our favor; we owe less to foreign countries than they owe to us; our industries are efficiently organized; our currency and bank deposits are protected by the greatest gold reserve in history.

Our first step toward recovery is to reestablish confidence and thus restore the flow of credit which is the very basis of our economic life. We must put some steel beams in the foundations of our credit structure. It is our duty to apply the full strength of our government not only to the immediate phases, but to provide security against shocks and the repetition of the weaknesses which have been proven.

The recommendations which I here lay before the Congress are designed to meet these needs by strengthening financial, industrial, and agricultural life through the medium of our existing institutions, and thus to avoid the entry of the Government into competition with private business.

FEDERAL GOVERNMENT FINANCE

The first requirement of confidence and of economic recovery is financial stability of the United States Government. I shall deal with fiscal questions at greater length in the Budget message. But I must at this time call attention to the magnitude of the deficits which have developed and the resulting necessity for determined and courageous policies. These deficits arise in the main from the heavy decrease in tax receipts due to the depression and to the increase in expenditure on construction in aid to unemployment, aids to agriculture, and upon services to veterans.

During the fiscal year ending June 30 last we incurred a deficit of about $903,000,000, which included the statutory reduction of the debt and represented an increase of the national debt by $616,000,000. Of this, however, $153,000,000 was offset by increased cash balances.

In comparison with the fiscal year 1928 there is indicated a fall in Federal receipts for the present fiscal year amounting to $1,683,000,000, of which $1,034,000,000 is in individual and corporate income taxes alone. During this fiscal year there will be an increased expenditure, as compared to 1928, on veterans of $255,000,000, and an increased expenditure on construction work which may reach $520,000,000. Despite large economies in other directions, we have an indicated deficit, including the statutory retirement of the debt, of $2,123,000,000, and an indicated net debt increase of about $1,711,000,000.

The Budget for the fiscal year beginning July 1 next, after allowing for some increase of taxes under the present laws and after allowing for drastic reduction in expenditures, still indicates a deficit of $1,417,000,000. After offsetting the statutory debt retirements this would indicate an increase in the national debt for the fiscal year 1933 of about $921,000,000.

Several conclusions are inevitable. We must have insistent and determined reduction in Government expenses. We must face a temporary increase in taxes. Such increase should not cover the whole of these deficits or it will retard recovery. We must partially finance the deficit by borrowing. It is my view that the amount of taxation should be fixed so as to balance the Budget for 1933 except for the statutory debt retirement. Such Government receipts would assure the balance of the following year's budget including debt retirement. It is my further view that the additional taxation should be imposed solely as an emergency measure terminating definitely two years from July 1 next. Such a basis will give confidence in the determination of the Government to stabilize its finance and will assure taxpayers of its temporary character. Even with increased taxation, the Government will reach the utmost safe limit of its borrowing capacity by the expenditures for which we are already obligated and the recommendations here proposed. To go further than these limits in either expenditures, taxes, or borrowing will destroy confidence, denude commerce and industry of their resources, jeopardize the financial system, and actually extend unemployment and demoralize agriculture rather than relieve it.

RECONSTRUCTION FINANCE CORPORATION

In order that the public may be absolutely assured and that the Government may be in position to meet any public necessity, I recommend that an emergency Reconstruction Corporation of the nature of the former War Finance Corporation should be established. It may not be necessary to use such an instrumentality very extensively. The very existence of such a bulwark will strengthen confidence. The Treasury should be authorized to subscribe a reasonable capital to it, and it should be given authority to issue its own debentures. It should be placed in liquidation at the end of two years. Its purpose is by strengthening the weak spots to thus liberate the full strength of the Nation's resources. It should be in postion to facilitate exports by American agencies; make advances to agricultural credit agencies where necessary to protect and aid the agricultural industry; to make temporary advances upon proper securities to established industries, railways, and financial institutions which can not otherwise secure credit, and where such advances will protect the credit structure and stimulate employment. Its functions would not overlap those of the National Credit Corporation.

FEDERAL RESERVE ELIGIBILITY

On October 6th I issued a statement that I should recommend to the Congress an extension during emergencies of the eligibility provisions in the Federal reserve act. This statement was approved by a representative gathering of the members of both Houses of the Congress, including members of the appropriate committees. It was approved by the officials of the Treasury Department, and I understand such an extension has been approved by a majority of the governors of the Federal reserve banks. Nothing should be done which would lower the safeguards of the system.

The establishment of the mortgage-discount banks herein referred to will also contribute to further reserve strength in the banks without inflation.

BANKING LAWS

Our people have a right to a banking system in which their deposits shall be safeguarded and the flow of credit less subject to storms. The need of a sounder system is plainly shown by the extent of bank failures. I recommend the prompt improvement of the banking laws. Changed financial conditions and commercial practices must be met. The Congress should investigate the need for separation between different kinds of banking; an enlargement of branch banking under proper restrictions; and the methods by which enlarged membership in the Federal reserve system may be brought about. . . .

UNEMPLOYMENT

As an aid to unemployment the Federal Government is engaged in the greatest program of public-building, harbor, flood-control, highway, waterway, aviation, merchant and naval ship construction in all history. Our expenditures on these works during this calendar year will reach about $780,000,000 compared with $260,000,000 in 1928. Through this increased construction, through the maintenance of a full complement of Federal employees, and through services to veterans it is estimated that the Federal taxpayer is now directly contributing to the livelihood of 10,000,000 of our citizens.

We must avoid burdens upon the Government which will create more unemployment in private industry than can be gained by further expansion of employment by the Federal Government. We can now stimulate employment and agriculture more effectually and speedily through the voluntary measures in progress, through the thawing out of credit, through the building up of stability abroad, through the home loan discount banks, through an emergency finance corporation and the rehabilitation of the railways and other such directions.

I am opposed to any direct or indirect Government dole. The breakdown and increased unemployment in Europe is due in part to such practices. Our people are providing against distress from unemployment in true American fashion by a magnificent response to public appeal and by action of the local governments.

CONCLUSION

It is inevitable that in these times much of the legislation proposed to the Congress and many of the recommendations of the Executive must be designed to meet emergencies. In reaching solutions we must not jeopardize those principles which we have found to be the basis of the growth of the Nation. The Federal Government must not encroach upon nor permit local communities to abandon that precious possession of local initiative and responsibility. Again, just as the largest measure of responsibility in the government of the Nation rests upon local self-government, so does the largest measure of social responsibility in our country rest upon the individual. If the individual surrenders his own initiative and responsibilities, he is surrendering his own freedom and his own liberty. It is the duty of the National Government to insist that both the local governments and the individual shall assume and bear these responsibilities as a fundamental of preserving the very basis of our freedom.

Many vital changes and movements of vast proportions are taking place in the economic world. The effect of these changes upon the future can not be seen clearly as yet. Of this, however, we are sure: Our system, based upon the ideals of individual initiative and of equality of opportunity, is not an artificial thing. Rather it is the outgrowth of the experience of America, and expresses the faith and spirit of our people. It has carried us in a century and a half to leadership of the economic world. If our economic system does not match our highest expectations at all times, it does not require revolutionary action to bring it into accord with any necessity that experience may prove. It has successfully adjusted itself to changing conditions in the past. It will do so again. The mobility of our institutions, the richness of our resources, and the abilities of our people enable us to meet them unafraid. It is a distressful time for many of our people, but they have shown qualities as high in fortitude, courage, and resourcefulness as ever in our history. With that spirit, I have faith that out of it will come a sounder life, a truer standard of values, a greater recognition of the results of honest effort, and a healthier atmosphere in which to rear our children. Ours must be a country of such stability and security

as can not fail to carry forward and enlarge among all the people that
abundant life of material and spiritual opportunity which it has represented among all nations since its beginning.

HERBERT HOOVER

The White House,
December 8, 1931

THE STIMSON DOCTRINE
January 7, 1932

*Secretary of State Henry L. Stimson, in identical notes to
Japan and China, declares that the United States will not
recognize any treaty or agreement impairing the political
independence or territorial integrity of China or adversely
affecting the Open Door policy. This declaration of non-
recognition was soon to be familiarly known as the Stimson Doctrine. Stimson sent the notes as a result of Japanese troops on September 18, 1931, marching into and
then occupying the Chinese province of Manchuria, using
as a reason an explosion on the South Manchurian Rail-
road. On October 16, 1931, Hoover announced that in this
crisis the United States would cooperate with the League
of Nations, which on December 10, 1931, appointed a
commission headed by the British Earl of Lytton to investigate the entire matter. The Lytton Commission published its report on October 4, 1932, condemning Japan
but also proposing that Manchuria become an autonomous
state under Chinese sovereignty but Japanese control.*

With the recent military operations about Chinchow, the last remaining administrative authority of the Government of the Chinese
Republic in South Manchuria, as it existed prior to September 18th,
1931, has been destroyed. The American Government continues confident that the work of the neutral commission recently authorized by
the Council of the League of Nations will facilitate an ultimate solution of the difficulties now existing between China and Japan.

But in view of the present situation and of its own rights and obligations therein, the American Government deems it to be its duty to
notify both the Imperial Japanese Government and the Government of
the Chinese Republic.

That it cannot admit the legality of any situation de facto nor does
it intend to recognize any treaty or agreement entered into between
those Governments, or agents thereof, which may impair the treaty
rights of the United States or its citizens in China, including those which
relate to the sovereignty, the independence, or the territorial and administrative integrity of the Republic of China, or to the international
policy relative to China, commonly known as the open door policy;

And that it does not intend to recognize any situation, treaty or agreement which may be brought about by means contrary to the covenants and obligations of the Pact of Paris of August 27, 1928, to which Treaty both China and Japan, as well as the United States, are parties.

ADDRESS TO THE SENATE ON A BALANCED BUDGET
May 31, 1932

In this address delivered in person to the Senate Hoover affirms that a balanced budget is necessary for ending the Depression and the return of national prosperity. His appearance before that body was the culmination of the declaration of a belief presented a number of times — both in spoken and written form, both in private and in public — that the passage of a balanced budget and national economic recovery were inextricably linked.

An emergency has developed in the last few days which it is my duty to lay before the Senate.

The continued downward movement in the economic life of the country has been particularly accelerated during the past few days and it relates in part definitely to the financial program of the Government. There can be no doubt that superimposed upon other causes the long continued delays in the passage of legislation providing for such reduction in expenses and such addition to revenues as would balance the Budget, together with proposals of projects which would greatly increase governmental expenditures, have given rise to doubt and anxiety as to the ability of our government to meet its responsibilities. These fears and doubts have been foolishly exaggerated in foreign countries. They know from bitter experience that the course of unbalanced budgets is the road of ruin. They do not realize that slow as our processes may be we are determined and have the resources to place the finances of the United States on an unassailable basis.

The immediate result has been to create an entirely unjustified run upon the American dollar from foreign countries and within the past few days despite our national wealth and resources and our unparalleled gold reserves our dollar stands at a serious discount in the markets of the world for the first time in half a century. This can be and must be immediately corrected or the reaction upon our economic situation will be such as to cause great losses to our people and will still further retard recovery. Nor is the confusion in public mind and the rising feeling of doubt and fear confined to foreign countries. It reflects itself directly in diminished economic activity and increased unemployment within our own borders and among our own citizens. There is thus further stress upon already diminished and strained economic life of the country.

No one has a more sympathetic realization than I of the difficulties and complexities of the problem with which the Congress is confronted. The decrease in revenues due to the depression by upwards of $1,700,000,000 and the consequent necessity to reduce Government expendi-

tures, the sacrifice such reduction calls for from many groups and
sections, the further sacrifice called for in the distribution of the remaining burden by the imposition of new taxes all constitute a problem
which naturally arouses wide divergence of sectional interest and individual views. Yet if we are to secure a just distribution of these sacrifices in such fashion as to establish confidence in the integrity of
the Government we must secure an adjustment of these views to
quick and prompt national action, directed at one sole purpose, that
is to unfetter the rehabilitation of industry, agriculture and employment. The time has come when we must all make sacrifices of some
parts of our particular views and bring these dangers and degenera-
tions to a halt by expeditious action.

In the stress of this emergency I have conferred with members of
both parties of the Senate as to methods by which the strains and
stresses could be overcome and the gigantic resources and energies
of our people released from the fetters in which they are held. I
have felt in the stress of this emergency a grave responsibility rests
upon me not only to present the situation to the Senate but to make suggestions as to the basis of adjustment between these views which I
hope will lead to early action. And I am addressing myself to the
Senate on this occasion as the major questions under consideration
are now before this body.

We have three major duties in legislation in order to accomplish
our fundamental purposes.

1. Drastic reduction of expenditures.

2. Passage of adequate revenue legislation, the combination of
which with reductions will unquestionably beyond all manner of doubt
declare to the world the balancing of the Federal Budget and the
stabilizing of the American dollar.

3. Passage of adequate relief legislation to assure the country
against distress and to aid in employment pending the next session of
Congress.

It is essential that when we ask our citizens to undertake the burdens of increased taxation we must give to them evidence of reduction
of every expenditure not absolutely vital to the immediate conduct of
the Government. The Executive Budget of last December provided for
a reduction of expenditures in the next fiscal year over the then estimated expenditures of the current year by about $370,000,000. I have
recommended to the Congress from time to time the necessity for
passage of legislation which would give authority for further important
reductions in expenditures not possible for consideration by either
the Executive or the Committees of Congress without such legislation.

An earnest non-partisan effort was made to secure these purposes
in a national economy bill in the House but it largely failed. That subject is under review by the bi-partisan committee appointed from the

members of the Senate Appropriations Committee and I am informed it has tentatively agreed upon a recommendation which would aggregate savings of $250,000,000 together with a number of undetermined further possibilities. I am not informed as to details of these recommendations, although I learn that my own suggestions in many instances have not been accepted. But I do know that the committee has made honest and earnest effort to reach a just reduction in expenditures and I trust therefore that, despite any of our individual views or the sacrifice of any group, we can unite in support and expeditious adoption of the committee's conclusions. In addition to the economies which may be brought about through the economy bill, the direct reductions of the appropriations committees should increase this figure to at least $400,000,000 not including certain postponements to later deficiency bills. As this sum forms the basis of calculations as to increased taxes necessary it is essential that no matter what the details may be, that amount of reduction must be obtained or taxes must be increased to compensate. If this minimum of $400,000,000 is attained by congressional action together with the $369,000,000 effected through the Executive Budget, except for amounts already budgeted for public works in aid to unemployment and increased costs of veterans, we will have reduced expenditures of this Government to the lowest point since 1916.

In the matter of tax legislation, we must face the plain and unpalatable fact that due to the degeneration in the economic situation during the past month the estimates of fertility of taxes which have been made from time to time based upon the then current prospects of business must be readjusted to take account of the decreasing business activity and shrinking values. The Finance Committee has been advised that the setbacks of the past month now make it evident that if we are to have absolute assurance of the needed income with breadth of base which would make a certainty of the collections we must face additional taxes to those now proposed by the Senate Finance Committee.

I recognize the complaint that estimates of the taxes required and reductions of expenses needed have been repeatedly increased, but on the other hand it should be borne in mind that if tax and economy legislation recommended from time to time since last December had been promptly enacted there would have been less degeneration and stagnation in the country. But it is unprofitable to argue any such questions. We must face the situation as it exists today.

In the course of the six months during which the revenue bill has been considered in the House and Senate practically every form of tax has been suggested at one time or another, many have found their way into the bill later to be rejected. The total amount Congress originally set out to obtain has been gradually whittled down either by actual reductions or degeneration of the situation while needs have increased.

If we examine the major sources of possible increases in taxes now proposed and the nature of taxes already voted, it may well be that the income taxes have already been raised to the point of diminishing returns through avoidance which will ensue by the use of tax-exempt securities and are already so high as to approach the danger point in retardation of enterprise. It is advisable that more relief should be given to earned incomes. Nor will further increase in income tax even including the proposals of Senator Connally cover the gap in our revenues or provide against any failure to reduce expenses to the full amount I have stated. The Senate has already imposed a multitude of specific manufacturers' excise taxes on special industries. Some of them appear discriminatory and uncertain in their productivity. I have not favored and do not favor a general sales tax. It has not been proposed by the Treasury. A sales tax is not, however, to be confused with an extension of the special manufacturers' excise taxes to a general manufacturers' excise tax with exemptions of food and clothing. This is an entirely different tax from a so-called sales tax and cannot be pyramided. Even this general manufacturers' excise tax has not been proposed by the Treasury, although at the time such a tax was unanimously recommended by the Ways and Means Committee of the House, representing both political parties and their leaders in the House of Representatives, the Secretary of the Treasury accepted it in the hope that immediate passage of the bill would result. In order, however, to solve our problem and give assurance to the country and the world of the impregnability of the American dollar and that we are ready to meet our emergencies at any sacrifice, I have now come to favor an extension for a limited period of the many special excise taxes to a more general manufacturers' excise tax and will support the Congress if it should be adopted. Whether this be the course or not some further emergency tax sources should be incorporated in the pending bill.

Our third problem is that of relief. The sharp degeneration has its many reflexes in distress and hardship upon our people. I hold that the maintenance of the sense of individual and personal responsibility of men to their neighbors and the proper separation of functions of the Federal and local governments requires the maintenance of the fundamental principle that the obligation of distress rests upon the individuals, upon the communities and upon the states. In order, however, that there may be no failure on the part of any state to meet its obligation in this direction I have, after consultation with some of the party leaders on both sides, favored authorization to the Reconstruction Finance Corporation to loan up to $300,000,000 to state governments where they are unable to finance themselves in provision of relief to distress. Such loans should be made by purchase of state bonds by the corporation but where states are unable to issue bonds then loans should be made upon application of state authorities and if they are not regularized by the issuance of bonds within a period of 12 to 18 months they should become a charge upon the Federal aid funds to which such states may be entitled.

In order to aid unemployment and to avoid wasteful expansion of public works I have favored an authority to the Reconstruction Corporation to increase its issues of its securities to the maximum of $3,000,000,000 in order that it may extend its services both in aid to employment and agriculture on a wide scale. Under the methods proposed the corporation is to be (a) authorized to buy bonds from political subdivisions or public bodies to aid in construction of income producing or self liquidating projects; (b) to make loans to established enterprise upon adequate security, for advancement of sound projects that will increase employment but safeguarded by requirement that some portion of outside capital is also provided; (c) to divert a portion of the unexpended authorizations of agricultural loans through the Secretary of Agriculture to finance the exports of agricultural products; (d) to make loans to institutions upon security of agricultural commodities and thus by stabilizing their loan value to steady their price levels; (e) to make loans to the Federal Farm Board to enable extension of finance of farm cooperatives.

I have not been able to favor the expansion of public works beyond the program already proposed in the Budget. I have for many years advocated speeding up of public works as relief to unemployment in times of depression. Since the beginning of this depression, in consonance with this view, the Federal Government will have expended in excess of $1,500,000,000 in construction and maintenance of one kind or another as against a normal program of perhaps $650,000,000 for a similar period. The Budget for next year calls for over $550,000,000 or double our usual outlay. If we shall now increase these programs we shall need instantly to increase taxes still further. We have already forced every project for which we have justification with any regard to the taxpayer and the avoidance of sheer waste. It is not my desire on this occasion to argue the comparative merits of extending such a program and that of financing an even larger program of employment on productive works through the Reconstruction Finance Corporation. We are indeed all desirous of serving our fellow citizens who are in difficulty and we must serve them in such a fashion that we do not increase the ranks of unemployed. I may emphasize that this alternative program avoids drain upon the taxpayer and above all if we are to balance our budget and balance it in such fashion that our people and the world may know it is balanced, we cannot make further appropriations in any direction beyond the amounts now before the Congress.

I am confident that if the Congress could find in these suggestions which come from members of both parties a ground for adjustment of legislation on those dominant particulars and could bring it into immediate action it would yield not only relief to the country but would reestablish that confidence which we so sorely need.

The natural wealth of this country is unimpaired and the inherent abilities of our people to meet their problems are being restrained by failure of the Government to act. Time is of the essence. Every day's delay makes new wounds and extends them. I come before you in sympathy with the difficulties which the problem presents and in a sincere spirit of helpfulness. I ask of you to accept such a basis of practical adjustment essential to the welfare of our people. In your hands at this moment is the answer to the question whether democracy has the capacity to act speedily enough to save itself in emergency. The Nation urgently needs unity. It needs solidarity before the world in demonstrating that America has the courage to look its difficulties in the face and the capacity and resolution to meet them.

FOURTH ANNUAL MESSAGE TO CONGRESS
December 6, 1932

In this message Hoover recommends to Congress that it take action to accomplish the following: the immediate and complete reorganization of the American banking system, the imposition of a special excise tax, a reorganization of the government through the grouping and consolidation of the more than 50 executive and independent agencies, a reduction of all government expenditures, the balancing of the budget.

To the Senate and House of Representatives:

In accord with my constitutional duty, I transmit herewith to the Congress information upon the state of the Union together with recommendation of measures for its consideration.

Our country is at peace. Our national defense has been maintained at a high state of effectiveness. All of the executive departments of the Government have been conducted during the year with a high devotion to public interest. There has been a far larger degree of freedom from industrial conflict than hitherto known. Education and science have made further advances. The public health is today at its highest known level. While we have recently engaged in the aggressive contest of a national election, its very tranquillity and the acceptance of its results furnish abundant proof of the strength of our institutions.

In the face of widespread hardship our poeple have demonstrated daily a magnificent sense of humanity, of individual and community responsibility for the welfare of the less fortunate. They have grown in their conceptions and organization for cooperative action for the common welfare.

In the provision against distress during this winter, the great private agencies of the country have been mobilized again; the generosity of our people has again come into evidence to a degree in which all America may take great pride. Likewise the local authorities and the states are engaged everywhere in supplemental measures of relief. The provisions made for loans from the Reconstruction Finance Corporation, to states that have exhausted their own resources, guarantee that there should be no hunger or suffering from cold in the country. The large majority of states are showing a sturdy cooperation in the spirit of the Federal aid.

The Surgeon General, in charge of the Public Health Service, furnishes me with the following information upon the state of public health:

Mortality rate per 1,000 of population on an annual basis
from representative States

First 9 months of	General	Infant
1928	11.9	67.8
1929	12.0	65.8
1930	11.4	62.0
1931	11.2	60.0
1932	10.6	55.0

The sickness rates from data available show the same trends. These facts indicate the fine endeavor of the agencies which have been mobilized for care of those in distress.

ECONOMIC SITUATION

The unparalleled world-wide economic depression has continued through the year. Due to the European collapse, the situation developed during last fall and winter into a series of most acute crises. The unprecedented emergency measures enacted and policies adopted undoubtedly saved the country from economic disaster. After serving to defend the national security, these measures began in July to show their weight and influence toward improvement of conditions in many parts of the country. The following tables of current business indicators show the general economic movement during the past eleven months.

Monthly business indices with seasonal variations eliminated
(Monthly average 1923–1925 = 100)

Year and Month	Industrial Production	Factory Employment	Freight-Car Loadings	Department Store Sales, Value	Exports, Value	Imports, Value	Building Contracts, All Types	Industrial Electric Power Consumption
1931								
December	74	69.4	69	81	46	48	38	89.1
1932								
January	72	68.1	64	78	39	42	31	93.9
February	69	67.8	62	78	45	41	27	98.8
March	67	66.4	61	72	41	37	26	88.0
April	63	64.3	59	80	38	36	27	82.2
May	60	62.1	54	73	37	34	26	82.0
June	59	60.0	52	71	34	36	27	78.1
July	58	58.3	51	67	32	27	27	79.2
August	60	58.8	51	66	31	29	30	73.5
September	66	60.3	54	70	33	32	30	84.0
October	66	61.1	57	70	33	32	29	84.4

The measures and policies which have procured this turn toward recovery should be continued until the depression is passed, and then the emergency agencies should be promptly liquidated. The expansion of credit facilities by the Federal Reserve System and the Reconstruction Finance Corporation has been of incalculable value. The loans of the latter for reproductive works, and to railways for the creation of employment; its support of the credit structure through loans to banks, insurance companies, railways, building and loan associations, and to agriculture has protected the savings and insurance policies of millions of our citizens and has relieved millions of borrowers from duress; they have enabled industry and business to function and expand. The assistance given to Farm Loan Banks, the establishment of the Home Loan Banks and Agricultural Credit Associations — all in their various ramifications have placed large sums of money at the disposal of the people in protection and aid. Beyond this, the extensive organization of the country in voluntary action has produced profound results.

The following table indicates direct expenditures of the Federal Government in aid to unemployment, agriculture, and financial relief over the past four years. The sums applied to financial relief multiply themselves many fold, being in considerable measure the initial capital supplied to the Reconstruction Finance Corporation, Farm Loan Banks, etc., which will be recovered to the Treasury.

	Public Works[1]	Agricultural Relief and Financial Loans
Fiscal year ending June 30 —		
1930	$410,420,000	$156,100,000
1931	574,870,000	196,700,000
1932	655,880,000	772,700,000
1933	717,260,000	52,000,000
Total	$2,358,430,000	$1,177,500,000

[1] Public Building, Highways, Rivers and Harbors and their maintenance, naval and other vessels construction hospitals, etc.

Continued constructive policies promoting the economic recovery of the country must be the paramount duty of the Government. The result of the agencies we have created and the policies we have pursued has been to buttress our whole domestic financial structure and greatly to restore credit facilities. But progress in recovery requires another element as well — that is fully restored confidence in the future. Institutions and men may have resources and credit but unless they have confidence progress is halting and insecure.

There are three definite directions in which action by the Government at once can contribute to strengthen further the forces of recovery by strengthening of confidence. They are the necessary foundations to any other action, and their accomplishment would at once promote employment and increase prices.

The first of these directions of action is the continuing reduction of all Government expenditures, whether national, state, or local. The difficulties of the country demand undiminished efforts toward economy in government in every direction. Embraced in this problem is the unquestioned balancing of the Federal Budget. That is the first necessity of national stability and is the foundation of further recovery. It must be balanced in an absolutely safe and sure manner if full confidence is to be inspired.

The second direction for action is the complete reorganization at once of our banking system. The shocks to our economic life have undoubtedly been multiplied by the weakness of this system, and until they are remedied recovery will be greatly hampered.

The third direction for immediate action is vigorous and whole-souled cooperation with other governments in the economic field. That our major difficulties find their origins in the economic weakness of foreign nations requires no demonstration. The first need today is strengthening of commodity prices. That can not be permanently accomplished by artificialities. It must be accomplished by expansion in consumption of goods through the return of stability and confidence in the world at large and that in turn can not be fully accomplished without cooperation with other nations.

BALANCING THE BUDGET

I shall in due course present the Executive Budget to the Congress. It will show proposed reductions in appropriations below those enacted by the last session of the Congress by over $830,000,000. In addition I shall present the necessary Executive orders under the recent act authorizing the reorganization of the Federal Government which, if permitted to go into force, will produce still further substantial economies. These sums in reduction of appropriations will, however, be partially offset by an increase of about $250,000,000 in uncontrollable items such as increased debt services, etc.

In the Budget there is included only the completion of the Federal public works projects already undertaken or under contract. Speeding up of Federal public works during the past four years as an aid to employment has advanced many types of such improvements to the point where further expansion can not be justified in their usefulness to the Government or the people. As an aid to unemployment we should beyond the normal constructive programs substitute reproductive or so-

called self-liquidating works. Loans for such purposes have been provided for through the Reconstruction Finance Corporation. This
change in character of projects directly relieves the taxpayer and is
capable of expansion into a larger field than the direct Federal works.
The reproductive works constitute an addition to national wealth and to
future employment, whereas further undue expansion of Federal public
works is but a burden upon the future.

The Federal construction program thus limited to commitments and
work in progress under the proposed appropriations contemplates
expenditures for the next fiscal year, including naval and other vessel
construction, as well as other forms of public works and maintenance,
of a total of $442,769,000, as compared with $717,262,000 for the present year.

The expenditure on such items over the four years ending June 30
next will amount to $2,350,000,000, or an amount of construction work
eight times as great as the cost of the Panama Canal and, except for
completion of certain long-view projects, places the Nation in many
directions well ahead of its requirements for some years to come. A
normal program of about $200,000,000 per annum should hereafter
provide for the country's necessities and will permit substantial future
reduction in Federal expenditures.

I recommend that the furlough system installed last year be continued not only because of the economy produced but because, being tanta-
mount to the "5-day week," it sets an example which should be followed
by the country and because it embraces within its workings the "spread
work" principle and thus serves to maintain a number of public ser-
vants who would otherwise be deprived of all income. I feel, however,
in view of the present economic situation and the decrease in the cost
of living by over 20 per cent, that some further sacrifice should be
made by salaried officials of the Government over and above the 8 1/3
per cent reduction under the furlough system. I will recommend that
after exempting the first $1,000 of salary there should be a temporary
reduction for one year of 11 per cent of that part of all Government
salaries in excess of the $1,000 exemption, the result of which, com-
bined with the furlough system, will average about 14.8 per cent reduction in pay to those earning more than $1,000.

I will recommend measures to eliminate certain payments in the
veterans' services. I conceive these outlays were entirely beyond the
original intentions of Congress in building up veterans' allowances.
Many abuses have grown up from ill-considered legislation. They should
be eliminated. The Nation should not ask for a reduction in allowances
to men and dependents whose disabilities rise out of war service nor
to those veterans with substantial service who have become totally
disabled from non-war-connected causes and who are at the same time
without other support. These latter veterans are a charge on the community at some point, and I feel that in view of their service to the

Nation as a whole the responsibility should fall upon the Federal Government.

Many of the economies recommended in the Budget were presented at the last session of the Congress but failed of adoption. If the Economy and Appropriations Committees of the Congress in canvassing these proposed expenditures shall find further reductions which can be made without impairing essential Government services, it will be welcomed both by the country and by myself. But under no circumstances do I feel that the Congress should fail to uphold the total of reductions recommended.

Some of the older revenues and some of the revenues provided under the act passed during the last session of the Congress, particularly those generally referred to as the nuisance taxes, have not been as prolific of income as had been hoped. Further revenue is necessary in addition to the amount of reductions in expenditures recommended. Many of the manufacturers' excise taxes upon selected industries not only failed to produce satisfactory revenue, but they are in many ways unjust and discriminatory. The time has come when, if the Government is to have an adequate basis of revenue to assure a balanced budget, this system of special manufacturers' excise taxes should be extended to cover practically all manufactures at a uniform rate, except necessary food and possibly some grades of clothing.

At the last session the Congress responded to my request for authority to reorganize the Government departments. The act provides for the grouping and consolidation of executive and administrative agencies according to major purpose, and thereby reducing the number and overlap and duplication of effort. Executive orders issued for these purposes are required to be transmitted to the Congress while in session and do not become effective until after the expiration of 60 calendar days after such transmission, unless the Congress shall sooner approve.

I shall issue such Executive orders within a few days grouping or consolidating over fifty executive and administrative agencies including a large number of commissions and "independent" agencies.

The second step, of course, remains that after these various bureaus and agencies are placed cheek by jowl into such groups, the administrative officers in charge of the groups shall eliminate their overlap and still further consolidate these activities. Therein lie large economies.

The Congress must be warned that a host of interested persons inside and outside the Government whose vision is concentrated on some particular function will at once protest against these proposals. These same sorts of activities have prevented reorganization of the Government for over a quarter of a century. They must be disregarded if the task is to be accomplished.

BANKING

The basis of every other and every further effort toward recovery is to reorganize at once our banking system. The shocks to our economic system have undoubtedly multiplied by the weakness of our financial system. I first called attention of the Congress in 1929 to this condition, and I have unceasingly recommended remedy since that time. The subject has been exhaustively investigated both by the committees of the Congress and the officers of the Federal Reserve System.

The banking and financial system is presumed to serve in furnishing the essential lubricant to the wheels of industry, agriculture, and commerce, that is, credit. Its diversion from proper use, its improper use, or its insufficiency instantly brings hardship and dislocation in economic life. As a system our banking has failed to meet this great emergency. It can be said without question of doubt that our losses and distress have been greatly augmented by its wholly inadequate organization. Its inability as a system to respond to our needs is today a constant drain upon progress toward recovery. In this statement I am not referring to individual banks or bankers. Thousands of them have shown distinguished courage and ability. On the contrary, I am referring to the system itself, which is so organized, or so lacking in organization, that in an emergency its very mechanism jeopardizes or paralyzes the action of sound banks and its instability is responsible for periodic dangers to our whole economic system.

Bank failures rose in 1931 to 10 1/2 per cent of all the banks as compared to 1 1/2 per cent of the failures of all other types of enterprise. Since January 1, 1930, we have had 4,665 banks suspend, with $3,300,000,000 in deposits. Partly from fears and drains from abroad, partly from these failures themselves (which indeed often caused closing of sound banks), we have witnessed hoarding of currency to an enormous sum, rising during the height of the crisis to over $1,600,000,000. The results from interreaction of cause and effect have expressed themselves in strangulation of credit which at times has almost stifled the Nation's business and agriculture. The losses, suffering, and tragedies of our people are incalculable. Not alone do they lie in the losses of savings to millions of homes, injury by deprival of working capital to thousands of small businesses, but also, in the frantic pressure to recall loans to meet pressures of hoarding and in liquidation of failed banks, millions of other people have suffered in the loss of their homes and farms, businesses have been ruined, unemployment increased, and farmers' prices diminished.

That this failure to function is unnecessary and is the fault of our particular system is plainly indicated by the fact that in Great Britain, where the economic mechanism has suffered far greater shocks than our own, there has not been a single bank failure during the depression. Again in Canada, where the situation has been in large degree identical with our own, there have not been substantial bank failures.

The creation of the Reconstruction Finance Corporation and the amendments to the Federal Reserve Act served to defend the Nation in a great crisis. They are not remedies; they are relief. It is inconceivable that the Reconstruction Corporation, which has extended aid to nearly 6,000 institutions and is manifestly but a temporary device, can go on indefinitely.

It is today a matter of satisfaction that the rate of bank failures, of hoarding, and the demands upon the Reconstruction Corporation have greatly lessened. The acute phases of the crisis have obviously passed and the time has now come when this national danger and this failure to respond to national necessities must be ended and the measures to end them can be safely undertaken. Methods of reform have been exhaustively examined. There is no reason now why solution should not be found at the present session of the Congress. Inflation of currency or governmental conduct of banking can have no part in these reforms. The Government must abide within the field of constructive organization, regulation, and the enforcement of safe practices only.

Parallel with reform in the banking laws must be changes in the Federal Farm Loan Banking system and in the Joint Stock Land Banks. Some of these changes should be directed to permanent improvement and some to emergency aid to our people where they wish to fight to save their farms and homes.

I wish again to emphasize this view—that these widespread banking reforms are a national necessity and are the first requisites for further recovery in agriculture and business. They should have immediate consideration as steps greatly needed to further recovery.

ECONOMIC COOPERATION WITH OTHER NATIONS

Our major difficulties during the past two years find their origins in the shocks from economic collapse abroad which in turn are the aftermath of the Great War. If we are to secure rapid and assured recovery and protection for the future we must cooperate with foreign nations in many measures.

We have actively engaged in a World Disarmament Conference where, with success, we should reduce our own tax burdens and the tax burdens of other major nations. We should increase political stability of the world. We should lessen the danger of war by increasing defensive powers and decreasing offensive powers of nations. We would thus open new vistas of economic expansion for the world.

We are participating in the formulation of a World Economic Conference, successful results from which would contribute much to advance in agricultural prices, employment, and business. Currency depreciation and correlated forces have contributed greatly to decrease in price levels. Moreover, from these origins rise most of the destructive trade barriers now stifling the commerce of the world. We could by successful action increase security and expand trade through stability in international exchange and monetary values. By such action world confidence could be restored. It would bring courage and stability, which would reflect into every home in our land.

The European governments, obligated to us in war debts, have requested that there should be suspension of payments due the United States on December 15 next, to be accompanied by exchange of views upon this debt question. Our Government has informed them that we do not approve of suspension of the December 15 payments. I have stated that I would recommend to the Congress methods to overcome temporary exchange difficulties in connection with this payment from nations where it may be necessary.

In the meantime I wish to reiterate that here are three great fields of international action which must be considered not in part but as a whole. They are of most vital interest to our people. Within them there are not only grave dangers if we fail in right action but there also lie immense opportunities for good if we shall succeed. Within success there lie major remedies for our economic distress and major progress in stability and security to every fireside in our country.

The welfare of our people is dependent upon successful issue of the great causes of world peace, world disarmament, and organized world recovery. Nor is it too much to say that today as never before the welfare of mankind and the preservation of civilization depend upon our solution of these questions. Such solutions can not be attained except by honest friendship, by adherence to agreements entered upon until mutually revised and by cooperation amongst nations in a determination to find solutions which will be mutually beneficial.

OTHER LEGISLATION

I have placed various legislative needs before the Congress in previous messages, and these views require no amplification on this occasion. I have urged the need for reform in our transportation and power regulation, in the antitrust laws as applied to our national resource industries, western range conservation, extension of Federal aid to child-health services, membership in the World Court, the ratification of the Great Lakes-St. Lawrence Seaway Treaty, revision of the bankruptcy acts, revision of Federal court procedure, and many other pressing problems.

These and other special subjects I shall where necessary deal with by special communications to the Congress.

The activities of our government are so great, when combined with the emergency activities which have arisen out of the world crisis, that even the briefest review of them would render the annual message unduly long. I shall therefore avail myself of the fact that every detail of the Government is covered in the reports to the Congress by each of the departments and agencies of the Government.

CONCLUSION

It seems to me appropriate upon this occasion to make certain general observations upon the principles which must dominate the solution of problems now pressing upon the Nation. Legislation in response to national needs will be effective only if every such act conforms to a complete philosophy of the people's purposes and destiny. Ours is a distinctive government with a unique history and background , consciously dedicated to specific ideals of liberty and to a faith in the inviolable sanctity of the individual human spirit. Furthermore, the continued existence and adequate functioning of our government in preservation of ordered liberty and stimulation of progress depends upon the maintenance of state, local, institutional, and individual sense of responsibility. We have builded a system of individualism peculiarly our own which must not be forgotten in any governmental acts, for from it have grown greater accomplishments than those of any other nation.

On the social and economic sides, the background of our American system and the motivation of progress is essentially that we should allow free play of social and economic forces as far as will not limit equality of opportunity and as will at the same time stimulate the initiative and enterprise of our people. In the maintenance of this balance the Federal Government can permit of no privilege to any person or group. It should act as a regulatory agent and not as a participant in economic and social life. The moment the Government participates, it becomes a competitor with the people. As a competitor it becomes at once a tyranny in whatever direction it may touch. We have around us numerous such experiences, no one of which can be found to have justified itself except in cases where the people as a whole have met forces beyond their control, such as those of the Great War and this great depression, where the full powers of the Federal Government must be exerted to protect the people. But even these must be limited to an emergency sense and must be promptly ended when these dangers are overcome.

With the free development of science and the consequent multitude of inventions, some of which are absolutely revolutionary in our national life, the Government must not only stimulate the social and economic responsibility of individuals and private institutions but it must also give leadership to cooperative action amongst the people which

will soften the effect of these revolutions and thus secure social trans-
formations in an orderly manner. The highest form of self-government is the voluntary cooperation within our people for such purposes.

But I would emphasize again that social and economic solutions,
as such, will not avail to satisfy the aspirations of the people unless
they conform with the traditions of our race, deeply grooved in their
sentiments through a century and a half of struggle for ideals of life
that are rooted in religion and fed from purely spiritual springs.

HERBERT HOOVER

The White House,
December 6, 1932

BIBLIOGRAPHICAL AIDS

BIBLIOGRAPHICAL AIDS

UNPUBLISHED PRIMARY SOURCES

The volume of unpublished primary sources relating to the long and varied career of Herbert Clark Hoover is considerable. However, scholars were denied access to the Hoover Papers by a prohibition steadfastly imposed by Hoover himself up to his death in 1964. Since then, scholars have been permitted to use the Hoover papers but have been hindered in their work by the restrictions placed upon the use of the material. Thus, until unfettered investigation into the primary sources is permitted, one cannot hope for works on Hoover that are characterized by a full and balanced analysis stemming from free and thorough research.

There are 2 main depositories of unpublished primary sources on Hoover: the Herbert Hoover Presidential Library in West Branch, Iowa, and the Hoover Institution on War, Revolution, and Peace at Stanford University.

The Herbert Hoover Presidential Library was dedicated by Hoover himself at his birthplace in 1962. It is under the supervision of the National Archives and Records Service. The bulk of the material in the Library previously formed the core of the Herbert Hoover Archives section of the Hoover Institution on War. Revolution, and Peace. The collection of Hoover papers on deposit in West Branch consists of the following: 1,100 boxes of papers from his term as President, 1929-33; 646 boxes of papers from his tenure as Secretary of Commerce, 1921-28; 14 boxes of papers from his tenure as Food Administrator, 1917-19; 1,700 boxes of papers pertaining to his career before entering government service as Food Administrator and after leaving it as President. In addition, the Library holds 128 boxes of records of the Commissions on the Organization of the Executive Branch of the Government of 1947-49 and of 1953-55 (familiarly known as the First and Second Hoover Commissions), plus 43 boxes of records of the American Child Health Association and 445 boxes of records of the Belgian-American Education Foundation, 2 organizations in which

Hoover took an active interest. Also on deposit are 325 boxes of the Lou Henry Hoover papers. As for secondary works, the Library maintains a body of some 4,000 books on the life and times of Hoover.

The Hoover Institution on War, Revolution, and Peace at Stanford University was founded in 1919. Located on the campus of Hoover's alma mater, the Institution contains materials on a variety of 20th century political, economic, and social problems, with special emphasis on the eras of World Wars I and II. Included in the holdings are 200,000 books, 26,000 bound periodical volumes, 40,000 maps and posters, and 3,500 reels of microfilm. On deposit in the Institution are the records of significant organizations of which Hoover was the head, such as the Commission for Relief in Belgium of 1914-17, which engaged in a program for the relief of Belgians and Frenchmen whose lands had been invaded by the German army, and the American Relief Administration of 1919, which engaged in the work of European food relief.

There are important unpublished primary source items on Hoover held by the following research centers: at the Library of Congress are the papers of Irwin Hood Hoover (no relation), the White House chief usher from 1909 to 1933, containing notebooks and diaries with observations on the Presidents, including Hoover; at the Yale University Library are the papers of Henry L. Stimson, Secretary of State during the Hoover Administration, containing a substantial number of letters from Hoover; at Princeton University Library are the papers of the New York banker Fred I. Kent containing correspondence with Hoover; at Harvard University Library are 57 letters of Hoover's from 1913 to 1947.

PRINTED HOOVER PAPERS

Myers, William S. (ed.). The State Papers and Other Public Writings of Herbert Hoover. 2 vols. Garden City, N.Y.: Doubleday, Doran & Company, Inc., 1934.

————, and Newton, Walter H. The Hoover Administration, A Documented Narrative. New York: Charles Scribner's Sons, 1936.

GOVERNMENT PUBLICATIONS

Report of the President's Conference on Unemployment, September 26 to October 13, 1921. Washington, D.C.: U.S. Government Printing Office, 1921.

U.S. Commission on Organization of the Executive Branch of the Government. Budgeting and Accounting, A Report to the Congress. Washington, D.C.: U.S. Government Printing Office, 1949.

U.S. Commission on Organization of the Executive Branch of the Government. The Independent Regulatory Commissions, A Report to the Congress. Washington, D.C.: U.S. Government Printing Office, 1949.

U.S. Commission on Organization of the Executive Branch of the Government. Office of General Services, A Report to the Congress. Washington, D.C.: U.S. Government Printing Office, 1949.

U.S. Commission on Organization of the Executive Branch of the Government. Reorganization of Federal Business Enterprises, A Report to the Congress. Washington, D.C.: U.S. Government Printing Office, 1949.

U.S. Commission on Organization of the Executive Branch of the Government. The Treasury Department, A Report to the Congress. Washington, D.C.: U.S. Government Printing Office, 1949.

U.S. Commission on Organization of the Executive Branch of the Government. The Hoover Commission Report on Organization of the Executive Branch of the Government. Washington, D.C.: U.S. Government Printing Office, 1955.

U.S. St. Lawrence Commission. St. Lawrence Waterway Project. Washington, D.C.: U.S. Government Printing Office, 1927.

WORKS BY HOOVER

Hoover, Herbert Clark. Addresses Upon the American Road, 1933-1938. New York: Charles Scribner's Sons, 1938.

————. Addresses Upon the American Road, 1940-1941. New York: Charles Scribner's Sons, 1941.

————. Addresses Upon the American Road, 1941-1945. New York: D. Van Nostrand Company, Inc., 1946.

————. Addresses Upon the American Road, 1945-1948. New York: D. Van Nostrand Company, Inc., 1949.

————. Addresses Upon the American Road, 1948-1950. Stanford: Stanford University Press, 1951.

————. Addresses Upon the American Road, 1950-1955. Stanford: Stanford University Press, 1955.

————. Addresses Upon the American Road, 1955-1960. Caldwell, Idaho: Caxton Printers, 1961.

————. An American Epic. 4 vols. Chicago: H. Regnery Co., 1959-60.

————. American Individualism. Garden City, N.Y.: Doubleday, Page & Company, 1922.

————. America's First Crusade. New York: Charles Scribner's Sons, 1942.

————, and Gibson, Hugh. The Basis of Lasting Peace. New York: D. Van Nostrand Company, Inc., 1945.

————. A Boyhood in Iowa. New York: Aventine Press, 1931.

————. The Challenge to Liberty. New York: Charles Scribner's Sons, 1934.

————, and Hoover, Lou Henry. De Re Metallica. London: The Mining Magazine, 1912.

————. Fishing for Fun — and to Wash Your Soul. New York: Random House, 1963.

————. Forty Key Questions about Our Foreign Policy. Scarsdale, N.Y.: Updegraff Press, 1952.

————. Further Addresses Upon the American Road. New York: Charles Scribner's Sons, 1940.

————. Memoirs. 3 vols. New York: The Macmillan Company, 1951-52.

————. The New Day, Campaign Speeches of Herbert Hoover, 1928. Stanford: University Press, 1928.

————. On Growing Up, Letters to American Boys and Girls. New York: William Morrow & Company, 1949.

————. The Ordeal of Woodrow Wilson. New York: McGraw-Hill Book Company, 1958.

————. Principles of Mining. New York: Hill Publishing Company, 1909.

————, and Gibson, Hugh. The Problems of Lasting Peace. Garden City, N.Y.: Doubleday, Doran & Company, Inc., 1942.

————. Shall We Send our Youth to War? New York: Coward-McCann, Inc., 1939.

————. The Vital Need for Greater Financial Support of Pure Science Research. Washington, D.C.: National Research Council, 1925.

MEMOIRS

Hoover, Irwin H. Forty-two Years in the White House. Boston: Houghton Mifflin Company, 1934.

Stimson, Henry L., and Bundy, McGeorge. On Active Service in Peace and War. New York: Harper & Brothers, 1947.

BIOGRAPHIES

Hinshaw, David. Herbert Hoover, American Quaker. New York: Farrar, Straus and Company, 1950.

Irwin, Will. Herbert Hoover, A Reminiscent Biography. New York: Century, 1928.

Lyons, Eugene. Herbert Hoover, A Biography. Garden City, N.Y.: Doubleday & Company, Inc., 1964.

————. Our Unknown Ex-President, A Portrait of Herbert Hoover. Garden City, N.Y.: Doubleday & Company, Inc., 1948.

Marsh, William John. Our President, Herbert Hoover. New Milford, Conn.: W.J. & C. Marsh, 1930.

Wilson, Carol. Herbert Hoover, A Challenge for Today. New York: Evans Publishing Co., 1968.

Wolfe, Harold. Herbert Hoover, Public Servant and Leader of the Loyal Opposition. New York: Exposition Press, 1956.

MONOGRAPHS

Asbury, Herbert. The Great Illusion, An Informal History of Prohibition. Garden City, N.Y.: Doubleday & Company, Inc., 1950.

Bane, Suda L., and Lutz, Ralph H. (eds.). Organization of American Relief in Europe, 1918-1919. Stanford: Stanford University Press, 1943.

Brandes, Joseph. Herbert Hoover and Economic Diplomacy, Department of Commerce Policy, 1921-1928. Pittsburgh: University of Pittsburgh Press, 1962.

Current, Richard N. Secretary Stimson, A Study in Statecraft. New Brunswick: Rutgers University Press, 1954.

Darling, Jay Norwood. As Ding Saw Hoover. Ames, Iowa: Iowa State College Press, 1954.

DeConde, Alexander. Herbert Hoover's Latin-American Policy. Stanford: Stanford University Press, 1951.

Dexter, Walter F. Herbert Hoover and American Individualism, A Modern Interpretation of a National Ideal. New York: The Macmillan Company, 1932.

Ferrell, Robert H. American Diplomacy in the Great Depression, Hoover-Stimson Foreign Policy, 1929-1933. New Haven: Yale University Press, 1957.

Galbraith, J. Kenneth. The Great Crash. Boston: Houghton Mifflin Company, 1954.

Gay, George I. The Commission for Relief in Belgium, A Statistical Review of Relief Operations. Stanford: Stanford University Press, 1925.

Lochner, Louis P. Herbert Hoover and Germany. New York: The Macmillan Company, 1960.

Merz, Charles. The Dry Decade. Garden City, N.Y.: Doubleday, Doran & Company, Inc., 1931.

Moore, Edmund A. A Catholic Runs for President, The Campaign of 1928. New York: Ronald Press Co., 1956.

Myers, William S. The Foreign Policies of Herbert Hoover, 1929-1933. New York: Charles Scribner's Sons, 1940.

Peel, Roy F., and Donnelly, Thomas C. The 1928 Campaign, An Analysis. New York: New York University Book Store, 1931.

_____. The 1932 Campaign, An Analysis. New York: Farrar & Rinehart, Inc., 1935.

Prothro, James W. The Dollar Decade, Business Ideas in the 1920's. Baton Rouge: Louisiana State University Press, 1954.

Romasco, Albert U. The Poverty of Abundance, Hoover, the Nation, the Depression. New York: Oxford University Press, 1965.

Sinclair, Andrew. Prohibition, The Era of Excess. Boston: Little, Brown and Company, 1962.

Smith, Sara R. The Manchurian Crisis, 1931-32, A Tragedy in International Relations. New York: Columbia University Press, 1948.

Surface, Frank M., and Bland, Raymond L. American Food in the World War and Reconstruction Period. Stanford: Stanford University Press, 1931.

Tugwell, Rexford G. Mr. Hoover's Economic Policy. New York: The John Day Company, 1932.

Warren, Harris G. Herbert Hoover and the Great Depression. New York: Oxford University Press, 1959.

Wilbur, Ray L., and Hyde, Arthur M. The Hoover Policies. New York: Charles Scribner's Sons, 1937.

Willis, Edward F. Herbert Hoover and the Russian Prisoners of World War I, A Study in Diplomacy and Relief, 1918-1919. Stanford: Stanford University Press, 1951.

GENERAL STUDIES

Freidel, Frank. Franklin D. Roosevelt, The Triumph. Vol. III. Boston: Little, Brown and Company, 1956.

Hicks, John D. Republican Ascendancy, 1921-1933. New York: Harper & Brothers, Publishers, 1960.

Hofstadter, Richard. The American Political Tradition And the Men Who Made It. New York: Alfred A. Knopf, 1948.

Mitchell, Broadus. Depression Decade, From New Era Through New Deal, 1929-1941. New York: Rinehart Company, 1947.

Schlesinger, Arthur M., Jr. The Age of Roosevelt, The Crisis of the Old Order, 1919-1933. Vol. I. Boston: Houghton Mifflin Company, 1957.

Schriftgiesser, Karl. This Was Normalcy. Boston: Little, Brown and Company, 1948.

Wecter, Dixon. The Age of the Great Depression, 1929-41. New York: The Macmillan Company, 1948.

OTHER BOOKS

Emerson, Edwin. Hoover and His Times, Looking Back Through the Years. Garden City, N.Y.: Garden City Publishing Company, Inc., 1932.

Guerrant, Edward O. Herbert Hoover, Franklin Roosevelt, Comparisons and Contrasts. Cleveland: H. Allen, 1960.

Hamill, John. The Strange Career of Mr. Hoover Under Two Flags. New York: W. Faro, Inc., 1931.

Hard, William. Who's Hoover? New York: Dodd, Mead and Company, 1928.

Joslin, Theodore G. Hoover Off the Record. Garden City, N.Y.: Doubleday, Doran & Company, Inc., 1934.

Knox, John. The Great Mistake. Washington, D.C.: National Foundation Press, Inc., 1930.

Lowry, Edward George. Washington Close-ups, Intimate Views of Some Public Figures. Boston: Houghton Mifflin Company, 1921.

Pringle, Henry F. Big Frogs. New York: Macy-Masins, 1928.

Train, Arthur Cheney. The Strange Attacks on Herbert Hoover, A Current Example of What We Do to Our Presidents. New York: The John Day Company, 1932.

NAME INDEX

THE PRESIDENTIAL CHRONOLOGIES

GEORGE WASHINGTON*
  edited by Howard F. Bremer
JOHN ADAMS*
  edited by Howard F. Bremer
THOMAS JEFFERSON **
  edited by Arthur Bishop
JAMES MADISON**
  edited by Ian Elliot
JAMES MONROE*
  edited by Ian Elliot
JOHN QUINCY ADAMS*
  edited by Kenneth Jones
ANDREW JACKSON**
  edited by Kenneth Jones
MARTIN VAN BUREN**
  edited by Irving J. Sloan
HARRISON/ TYLER***
  edited by David A. Durfee
JAMES K. POLK*
  edited by John J. Farrell
TAYLOR/ FILLMORE**
  edited by John J. Farrell
THEODORE ROOSEVELT**
  edited by Gilbert Black
WILLIAM HOWARD TAFT*
  edited by Gilbert Black
WOODROW WILSON**
  edited by Robert I. Vexler
FRANKLIN PIERCE*
  edited by Irving J. Sloan
JAMES BUCHANAN*
  edited by Irving J. Sloan
ABRAHAM LINCOLN***
  edited by Ian Elliot
ANDREW JOHNSON*
  edited by John N. Dickinson

ULYSSESS S. GRANT**
  edited by Philip R. Moran
RUTHERFORD B. HAYES*
  edited by Arthur Bishop
GARFIELD/ ARTHUR***
  edited by Howard B. Furer
GROVER CLEVELAND**
  edited by Robert I. Vexler
BENJAMIN HARRISON*
  edited by Harry J. Sievers
WILLIAM McKINLEY*
  edited by Harry J. Sievers
WARREN G. HARDING**
  edited by Philip R. Moran
CALVIN COOLIDGE***
  edited by Philip R. Moran
HERBERT HOOVER*
  edited by Arnold Rice
FRANKLIN D. ROOSEVELT****
  edited by Howard F. Bremer
HARRY S TRUMAN***
  edited by Howard B. Furer
DWIGHT D. EISENHOWER***
  edited by Robert I. Vexler
JOHN F. KENNEDY*
  edited by Ralph A. Stone
LYNDON B. JOHNSON***
  edited by Howard B. Furer

    *   96 pages, $3.00
  ** 128 pages, $4.00
 *** 160 pages, $5.00
**** 224 pages, $7.00